Agatha Christie: A Very Short Introduction

VERY SHORT INTRODUCTIONS are for anyone wanting a stimulating and accessible way into a new subject. They are written by experts, and have been translated into more than 45 different languages.

The series began in 1995, and now covers a wide variety of topics in every discipline. The VSI library currently contains over 750 volumes—a Very Short Introduction to everything from Psychology and Philosophy of Science to American History and Relativity—and continues to grow in every subject area.

Very Short Introductions available now:

Available soon:

For more information visit our website

www.oup.com/vsi/

Gill Plain

AGATHA CHRISTIE

A Very Short Introduction

OXFORD
UNIVERSITY PRESS

Great Clarendon Street, Oxford, OX2 6DP,
United Kingdom

Oxford University Press is a department of the University of Oxford.
It furthers the University's objective of excellence in research, scholarship,
and education by publishing worldwide. Oxford is a registered trade mark of
Oxford University Press in the UK and in certain other countries

Published in the United States of America by Oxford University Press
198 Madison Avenue, New York, NY 10016, United States of America

British Library Cataloguing in Publication Data
Data available

Library of Congress Control Number: 2025930595

ISBN 9780198863748

DOI: 10.1093/9780191896095.001.0001

Printed and bound by
CPI Group (UK) Ltd., Croydon, CR0 4YY

Links to third party websites are provided by Oxford in good faith and
for information only. Oxford disclaims any responsibility for the materials
contained in any third party website referenced in this work.

The manufacturer's authorised representative in the EU for product safety is Oxford University
Press España S.A. of El Parque Empresarial San Fernando de Henares,
Avenida de Castilla, 2 – 28830 Madrid (www.oup.es/en or product.safety@oup.com).
OUP España S.A. also acts as importer into Spain of products made by the manufacturer.

Contents

Preface

The scene is a village. Its population, always small, is now even smaller, as someone has been murdered. Due to inclement weather, poor transport links, and serendipitous timing, one of only a handful of people could have done it. All of them wanted to. The police are baffled: but all is not lost. Conveniently on the scene or close at hand we find a detached figure with clinical powers of observation, a duty to the truth, a total absence of sentiment, and a fundamental belief that there is nothing new under the sun. We can relax. All will be explained. We are in the perversely safe hands of Agatha Christie.

Acknowledgements

This book owes a considerable debt to the students on my crime fiction courses at the University of St Andrews. It's been a pleasure talking about Christie with them, and I'm grateful for the many insights I've accumulated over the years. Particular thanks to Ella Geraghty, Karoline Strauch, and Benjamin Parris, whose observations—on actresses, eugenics, and the darker side of Hercule Poirot—all prompted me to think afresh, and to the recent class who introduced me to the world of Agatha Christie video games. I have no intention of playing them, but am delighted to know they exist.

I'm grateful to Agatha Christie Limited and to HarperCollins for permission to quote from published work, and to the Christie Archive Trust and Special Collections at the University of Exeter for access to the fascinating archive of Christie's Business Papers. At Oxford University Press I owe huge thanks to Luciana O'Flaherty and Imogene Haslam for their patience and support throughout the surprisingly long time it has taken to write a short introduction. During this time, and before, there have also been countless Christie conversations with colleagues, friends, and crime connoisseurs. There isn't space to name everyone, but thanks to Jamie Bernthal, Clare Collins, Katie Garner, Megan Hoffman, Kerstin Anja Münderlein, Fiona Peters, Anindya

Raychaudhuri, Caroline Reitz, Susan Sellers, Victoria Stewart, Emma Sutton, and Ben Winsworth. Special mention to Petra Rau for vital help at the planning stage and to Kaite O'Reilly for a grand day out at the theatre. This is for James McKinna, for keeping me company through so many adaptations.

Agatha Christie

List of illustrations

Chapter 1
Agatha Christie and the 'Golden Age' of crime

To call Agatha Christie a bestseller is an understatement. The author of over 80 books and the world's longest running play, she has been translated into over 100 languages and some two billion copies of her works have been sold. Yet this astonishing achievement begs a simple question: why? What is it about Christie's writing, her characters, plots, and settings that have made her not just nationally, but globally, enduring? Why did the detective stories of a middle-class, middlebrow Englishwoman appeal to such a broad range of readers? Why, indeed, do they continue to appeal? In this first chapter, I introduce Christie, as a writer and as a woman whose life would span three-quarters of the 20th century, with all the social, cultural, and political transitions that implies. Christie was born a Victorian and died under the auspices of the welfare state. In between, she survived two world wars and a raft of social change running from women's enfranchisement to the abolition of the death penalty. She also played a central role in crime fiction's evolution into the 20th century's most popular genre. Christie grew up alongside the 'clue-puzzle' formula and manipulated it with unparalleled efficiency across the five decades of her writing career. In the second part of this chapter, I consider the range and influence of that formula, and its significance within 20th-century culture.

Who was Agatha Christie?

> She was a lucky woman who had established a happy knack of writing what quite a lot of people wanted to read. (*Elephants Can Remember*, chapter 1)

To get a sense of Christie's personality, her pleasures, politics, and prejudices, there is no better source than her *Autobiography*, started in 1950 and finally completed some 15 years later, at the age of 75. The book is meandering and conversational—explosions of memory vividly recalled and loosely structured into a life's progression. It is a story retold with relish: a vibrant recreation of a Victorian childhood and 20th-century woman's life, mapping social interaction, the textures of domesticity, the adventure of travel, and the pleasures of food. Yet it is equally a masterclass in unreliable narration that enjoys the autobiographer's privilege of selective memory. For readers desiring a little more accuracy, and some insight into the difficulties of Christie's life—the hurts she carefully excludes from her own account—there are three substantial biographies from which to choose. Janet Morgan, the first authorized biographer, writing less than 10 years after Christie's death, provides a crisp and readable account, enriched by direct access to many of those who knew Christie best. Morgan also succinctly captures the forces—social, historical, familial—that shaped the writer and her work. Laura Thompson, writing over 20 years later, takes a different approach, drawing on the autobiographical dimension of Christie's fiction to create a more intimate, if speculative, picture. Most recently, the historian Lucy Worsley has approached the subject with a broader brush, summarizing the work of her predecessors to enable a focus on Christie's radical duality: her ability to break boundaries while hiding in plain sight behind the façade of 'ordinary' womanhood. Unless otherwise indicated, my quotations come from the *Autobiography*.

Christie was born in the seaside town of Torquay on 15 September 1890, some years after her sister Madge (1879), and brother 'Monty' (1880). Her father, Frederick Miller, was a well-to-do American man of leisure, happy to live off his trust funds until the dividends somewhat mysteriously dried up. Her mother, Clara Boehmer, was a more dynamic figure. Described in the *Autobiography* as an 'enigmatic and arresting personality', she was fascinated by ideas—particularly as manifest in religion—and would be a huge influence on her daughter. Christie's early years were happy: she was, Laura Thompson perceptively suggests, 'in love with her own childhood' and, safe in the gardens of Ashfield, her comfortable middle-class home, she built elaborate narratives around a collection of toys and imaginary friends. It was an idyllic Victorian existence, until her father's financial problems and his increasing ill-health began to cast shadows over the family. In 1896 they wintered in France for economy, the rent from the immense space of Ashfield covering their expenses. During this extended stay, Agatha first encountered French, and although she would eventually become fluent, her acquisition of a second language was as haphazard as the rest of her education. Without formal schooling, she nonetheless taught herself to read, and voraciously consumed the family's diverse bookshelves.

It is tempting, given Christie's reputation as the 'queen' of a particularly English mode of domestic murder, to overlook the cosmopolitan nature of her upbringing. After her father's death in 1901, her secure and ordered world admitted new anxieties and considerably greater economies. These factors, plus a transition in her mother's views on education, determined a late departure for school in France. Here Agatha excelled at music, becoming a skilled pianist and singer, dreaming briefly of a professional career before performance anxiety and the limited strength of her voice defeated her. In the end, the more conventional 'career' of marriage beckoned, although a London season could not be afforded. Instead, mother and daughter departed for Cairo. As a 'finishing' strategy, this was clearly successful and by the time Agatha met the young army subaltern, Archie Christie, she was already the veteran of several plausible marriage proposals. As described in the *Autobiography*, Archie was of a different order to her previous suitors—emotionally volatile, unpredictable, 'a stranger'—someone whose moods and opinions Agatha could not anticipate. She recalls, without comment, that he 'had the happy attitude of going through life without the least interest in what anyone thought of him or his belongings: his mind was always entirely bent on what he wanted himself'. This perhaps encapsulates why, ultimately, the marriage failed, but in 1912, it was Agatha's first experience of intense, all-consuming desire. Neither party could afford to marry immediately, so it was not until Christmas Eve 1914, with the country at war and Archie in the newly formed Royal Flying Corps (RFC), that a chaotic, last-minute ceremony took place.

While Archie pursued his successful (albeit grounded) career in the RFC, Agatha returned home and joined a Voluntary Aid Detachment (VAD), becoming a hastily trained 'civilian' nurse within the military hospital system. This was, as she describes it, a life-changing experience, and for all the horror of the wards, she felt she might have had a vocation for nursing. Instead, when she was redeployed to the hospital dispensary, the seeds of a very different career took root. Here, in 1916, in the quiet hours of her shifts, she mapped out her first detective story. *The Mysterious Affair at Styles*—the book that would introduce Hercule Poirot to the world—would not find a publisher until 1920, when John Lane took it at terms highly disadvantageous to the fledgling author. This might have been a case of an experienced publisher recognizing 'an easy touch when he saw one', but at the time, Christie did not care; she was, as the *Autobiography* recalls, 'the complete amateur… For me, writing was fun.' In between composition and publication, much had happened. With the war finally over, and Archie a colonel, married life together became possible; but money remained tight—a situation exacerbated by the birth, in August 1919, of their daughter Rosalind. Keeping up middle-class appearances was a challenge and Archie encouraged Agatha to write more novels. The first Tommy and Tuppence story, *The Secret Adversary* (1922), and the second Poirot, *Murder on the Links* (1923), followed in quick succession. In this phase of Christie's life, the *Autobiography* becomes a fascinating social history, detailing the young couple's struggle to find accommodation on their limited income for a household comprising parents, daughter, maid, and nanny. As Morgan wryly observes, for the middle classes of the 1920s cars were an extravagance, servants were not.

The next formative shift in Christie's life came through remarkable good fortune: Archie was invited to join the British Empire Exhibition Mission—a year-long voyage embracing South Africa, Australia, New Zealand, Canada, and New York, with a holiday in Honolulu thrown in for good measure. Christie was already an enthusiastic traveller, and this was an opportunity not to be missed. Leaving Rosalind in the care of her mother and sister, the two departed on an expedition that was less idyllic than advertised but nonetheless life changing. Yet, when they returned to Britain, Archie struggled to find work, and it was in these years that Christie first began to think of her writing in more professional terms. She found an agent, Edmund Cork, who would support her loyally, looking after her affairs, and those of her literary estate, until his death in 1988. Alongside introducing Christie to the lucrative world of serial rights, he negotiated improved contractual terms with a new publisher, Collins, initiating another relationship that would last Christie's lifetime. Christie's first book for Collins was *The Murder of Roger Ackroyd* (1926), a hugely successful tour de force, the solution to which remains amongst Christie's most admired. With Archie now comfortably employed in the city, everything was going swimmingly—a situation Christie summarizes in unexpected terms: 'I ought to have felt misgiving. Things went too well.' In short order, Christie's mother died, leaving her bereft as she attempted to clear out Ashfield; Archie, declining to help, fell in love with another woman during her absence; the marriage broke down; she 'disappeared'—an event that has been the subject of conjecture since 1926—and she was left a single parent, short of cash, and obliged to make the complete transition from amateur to professional writer. The *Autobiography* is at its most evasive in this section of her life. The couple had moved to Sunningdale, in Berkshire, catering to Archie's growing golf obsession, and it is through golf—imagined as religion or addiction—that Christie symbolically configures the breakdown of her marriage. Her approach to Archie's infidelity once again evokes the idea of him as a stranger, but this time the distance is far from exciting. Archie, while not directly criticized, comes across as childish and solipsistic: 'I can't stand not having what I want, and I can't stand not being happy.'

As indicated above, much has been written about Christie's 'disappearance': 11 days in which a desolately unhappy Agatha went missing, setting in motion an immense police search, newspaper saturation coverage, and even questions in Parliament. On Friday, 3 December 1926, at around 11.00 p.m., Christie drove away from her home in Sunningdale. Her car was later found abandoned at Newlands Corner in Surrey. What happened after that is almost impossible to discern, but Christie's biographers have done their best to construct a narrative from the fragments of evidence. Morgan succinctly parses the contradictions of witnesses before concluding that 'wishful thinking, zealous speculation and irrelevance dog the whole of this unhappy story'. Thompson tells the tale from Christie's point of view, suspecting her, at some possibly subconscious level, of attempting to punish Archie. She draws heavily on Christie's fictions of obsessive love to imagine her state of mind, and both writers support the idea of some form of breakdown generated by grief, illness, exhaustion, and unhappiness. Lucy Worsley joins Morgan in considering some form of 'dissociative fugue' and suggests a 'half-hearted attempt to take her life'. Beyond these careful biographies, speculation abounds—just as it did at the time, when press and police theories ranged from suicide to murder to a publicity stunt. Jared Cade describes a revenge plot that spiralled out of control when the investigation failed to respond as anticipated. The claims of amnesia, he suggests, were a cover up by Archie, determined to protect his mistress, Nancy Neele. The film *Agatha* (1979) constructs a brief encounter between Vanessa Redgrave's Christie and an American journalist (Dustin Hoffman), in which he eventually saves her from a suicide attempt. In *The Christie Affair* (2022), novelist Nina de Gramont opts for a more extravagantly romantic solution, imagining Christie on the run with the Irish former lover of Archie's mistress. More extravagant still, the television series *Dr Who* sent Christie to assist the Doctor in a battle against a giant alien wasp. Whatever actually happened, Christie was eventually discovered in a Harrogate hotel, seemingly suffering from amnesia. The publicity—exacerbated by the fervid speculations and unresolved questions of the past week—was horrific, and she took refuge with her sister before receiving treatment from a Harley Street psychiatrist.

The far side of what Thompson calls the 'great rupture of 1926', Christie took to travelling again, and made the fortuitous decision to head to Baghdad. Here she met the renowned archaeologist Leonard Woolley and his wife Katharine, who introduced her, a year later, to his ambitious young assistant Max Mallowan. Although 14 years her junior, Mallowan would become Christie's second husband and, according to the *Autobiography*, he decided she was the woman for him when, stuck in the desert in a potentially dangerous situation, Christie curled up in the shade and went to sleep. This complete absence of *'fuss'* was an inspiration to Max, and the two were married discreetly in Edinburgh in September 1930. Christie writes of the relationship in terms of friendship and common interests: Max's work appealed far more to her than 'Archie's deals in the City', and it undoubtedly brought adventure. Across the 1930s, the couple travelled widely, not just mapping conventional routes between Britain, Iran, and Syria, but also taking a detour to the USSR. Enthused by archaeology, Christie threw herself into supporting her new husband's career, helping on digs in Ur and Nineveh, and backing Mallowan's decision to strike out on his own with a solo dig at Arpachiyah in Iraq. Christie would continue her own work on expeditions, but also provided hands-on support, cleaning, recording, and photographing artefacts. She would later write warmly of this period in one of her few non-fiction books, the memoir *Come, Tell Me How You Live* (1946). Across the 1930s, Christie wrote prolifically, mostly about Poirot, but also—in *The Murder at the Vicarage* (1930)—introducing Miss Jane Marple, the detective who would be central to the second half of her career. Her work sold well in both Britain and America, her reputation grew, and life was, relatively speaking, 'free of outside shadows'.

The same cannot be said of what followed: the exhausting, stressful years of the Second World War. After the initial anticlimactic hiatus of the 'phoney war', Christie entered a period of frantic activity and domestic dislocation. With Max in the RAF and, ultimately, North Africa, and her Devon home Greenway requisitioned by the Admiralty, Christie commenced a nomadic life shuttling between various London residences and Pwllywrach in Wales, where Rosalind had moved after marrying an army major, Hubert Prichard. During this time, she also resumed her dispensing career, entered one of the most energetic phases of her writing life—producing roughly two books a year alongside radio and stage plays—and became a grandmother. Rosalind's son Mathew was born in September 1943; his father was killed in action in August 1944. The physical and psychological pressure of these years cannot be underestimated, and Christie writes perceptively of how the anticipation of disaster became a perverse normality:

So time went on, now not so much like a nightmare as something that had always been going on, had *always* been there. It had become, in fact, natural to expect that you yourself might be killed soon, that the people you loved best might be killed, that you would hear of deaths of friends. Broken windows, bombs, landmines, and in due course flying-bombs and rockets—all these things would go on, not as something extraordinary, but as perfectly natural...You could not really envisage a time when there would not be a war any more.

As if war, loneliness, and bereavement were not enough, this was also a period of considerable financial difficulty for Christie. She had fallen foul of changing American tax laws and incurred a terrifying debt, which was exacerbated by the complexities of wartime currency regulations. The correspondence between Edmund Cork and her American agent Harold Ober reveals a Kafkaesque situation in which Christie was expected to pay income tax on money she had not received, and—in due course—to face further taxation from the British authorities when the money finally arrived. The situation was not regularized until 1954, and it is a short imaginative journey from this persistent pressure to the complaints about bureaucracy that find expression in novels such as *Taken at the Flood* (1948).

When the dislocations of war finally came to an end, the exhausted but nonetheless resilient Christie reclaimed Greenway from the Admiralty, resumed her support of Max's career—travelling to Nimrud, the dig that would make him famous—and became for a while the doyenne of the London stage. She had first turned to the form in the 1930s, out of frustration at early adaptations of her work, and she proved adept at converting her fiction into drama. Morgan notes her sure touch in this new medium. Her plays were well-structured, plot-driven dramas: 'intellectually demanding but safe'. Theatre historian Julius Green puts it more trenchantly, describing Christie as 'the most successful female playwright of all time' before wryly noting that she 'also wrote some books'. Christie's claim to this title is evident not only from *The Mousetrap*—the world's longest running play, first performed in 1952 and still playing at the St Martin's Theatre in London—but also from her dominance of West End Theatre in the 1940s and 1950s, with successes such as *And Then There Were None* (1943), *Witness for the Prosecution* (1953), and *Spider's Web* (1954), a star vehicle for Margaret Lockwood, one of Britain's most popular film stars. *Witness for the Prosecution* also took Broadway by storm. With glowing reviews, a run of 645 performances and Tony awards for two of its actors, it earned Christie the New York Drama Critics Circle Award for Best Foreign Play. Christie loved the theatre and kept writing for it even as tastes changed in the wake of the 1956 Royal Court 'revolution', which saw the so-called 'well-made play' usurped by 'angry' young dramatists writing kitchen-sink realism. Her final West End hit would be *The Unexpected Guest* (1958), but her work has never gone out of fashion with amateur groups and repertory companies.

The 1950s also brought other pleasures. Much to Christie's delight, Rosalind remarried, and her new husband, Anthony Hicks, would become a mainstay of the household. Christie also continued to enjoy the conviviality of Max's expeditions, which she supported financially, emotionally, and practically. Worsley notes that she discreetly topped up his university salary and stepped in when Nimrud sponsorship dried up; she also presided over the dig's domestic arrangements and kept on writing to ensure a steady stream of income for them both. The rhythms of this archaeological and literary marriage only changed towards the end of the decade. The 1958 revolution in Iraq, while not quite ending Max's work, hastened its demise. An expedition that had been, in Worsley's words, a 'tentacle of British soft power in the region', had—like much of Britain's global influence—run its course, and it would be Iraqi archaeologists who would take over the excavation. Equally, Christie's good-humoured willingness to sleep in tents was increasingly at odds with what was physically possible for her now she had reached her late sixties. The Mallowans returned home for good, where Max worked on his magnum opus, *Nimrud and Its Remains*. The book was published in 1966 and he was knighted in 1968.

Given Agatha Christie's phenomenal success, it seems, with hindsight, a little odd that her much younger husband should be knighted before she was made a Dame of the British Empire in 1971. Yet this is, in other respects, entirely consonant with Christie's view of the world. Throughout her life, Christie maintained an ambivalent relationship towards her status as a professional writer, seemingly preferring the role of 'married woman'. Yet this self-effacing rejection of the designation 'author' and the concept of a 'career' must be set against evidence that she took her job very seriously indeed. Even in the 1930s we find her modest assurance that she can write anywhere accompanied by a firm insistence on her professional needs—as, for example, at Nineveh, where she overcame excavation director Campbell Thompson's parsimony to argue for a table of her own. Her business papers similarly illustrate how seriously she took the presentation and marketing of her work. She had very strong feelings about cover designs and if not appropriately consulted could explode at her publishers, usually via the resilient and emollient Edmund Cork. But while Collins became increasingly deferential, Christie's anger found new—and justifiable—focus in the 1960s when her work became a sought-after multi-media commodity. A deal with MGM that saw Miss Marple transformed out of all recognition, and tried to turn Poirot into a tough guy, proved genuinely distressing for Christie, who felt her creations had been abused and her work travestied.

From the 1940s, if not before, Christie's name carried weight, a weight that she found increasingly troublesome, and which speaks to a growing gulf between the woman who wrote and the commodities she produced. Christie was an internationally bestselling housewife who loved theatre culture but liked nothing better than to travel incognito. These states were irreconcilable, and the division between private and public was eventually concretized in 1955 with the creation of 'Agatha Christie Ltd'. The main reason for the decision was the need to rationalize Christie's convoluted tax position, but it also effected a symbolic divide between person and product. Christie became a waged employee working for the company producing her literary work. In the long term this helped render her financial affairs manageable, but the company, and the efforts of her agents Cork and Ober, could only do so much to ward off the attentions of a world that wanted more. Christie, who loathed publicity, reflected on this in her postwar fiction—often through her fictional avatar, the successful detective novelist Mrs Ariadne Oliver, who is regularly used for the purposes of self-parody. In *Mrs McGinty's Dead* (1952), for example, Mrs Oliver is tormented by a 'clever' young man who wants to adapt her fiction for the stage. In agony, she listens to his plans to turn her 60-year-old Finnish detective, who has 'never cared for women', into an amorous 35-year-old member of the Norwegian Resistance (chapters 10 and 12). The experience is exhausting, and she drifts wistfully into a 'nostalgic dream of home': 'A deal table, her typewriter, black coffee, apples everywhere...What bliss, what glorious and solitary bliss! What a mistake for an author to emerge from her secret fastness. Authors were shy, unsociable creatures, atoning for their lack of social aptitude by inventing their own companions and conversations' (chapter 17).

Mrs Oliver makes comedy out of a situation that frustrated Christie, who, while never short of ideas, felt the pressure of her position as the engine of the company. She also mourned the loss of the 'direct' relationship between writing and money she had once so enjoyed, and there is a desolate recognition of lost control in the later stages of the *Autobiography*: 'I often feel that it might be as well if I never wrote another word, because if I do it will only make further complications.' Yet for all her anxieties, Christie remained creative and energetic throughout her seventies. Her biographers note the pleasure she took in music—especially Wagner—in sumptuous food, and in an equally rich palate of reading. She consumed contemporary fiction from Gerald Durrell to Muriel Spark, thrillers by Alistair MacLean and Hammond

Innes, eclectic volumes of history and the Fontana Modern Masters, a series whose initial run included Fanon, Chomsky, and Wittgenstein. Morgan suggests she retained a lifelong enthusiasm for intellectual speculation, and although her writing changed in the last decade of her life, she took her readers with her. So much so that her final completed novel, *Postern of Fate* (1973), confounded the expectations of family, agents, and publishers by achieving good reviews and excellent sales. Yet the novel does, undoubtedly, bear signs of decline. Featuring a final outing for Tommy and Tuppence Beresford, it is more an exercise in nostalgia than a crime novel. Indeed, the book spends as much time recapping Christie's childhood and the Beresfords' old adventures as it does developing the plot of their new 'investigation'. Morgan's early biography notes her physical and mental deterioration, and the efforts of the family to protect her; Worsley cites recent research that suggests Christie had developed Alzheimer's disease. She died on 12 January 1976, shortly after the publication of the last Poirot novel, *Curtain* (1975), and before the last Marple, *Sleeping Murder* (1976), both of which had been written and stashed away for security in the anxious years of the 1940s.

Between 1920 and 1976, then, a private young woman writing for pleasure became the public phenomenon, 'Agatha Christie'. As her biographers agree, this was a challenging transition, and the desire to explore ideas beyond the expectations of her burgeoning criminal career contributed to the development of another alter ego. Between 1930 and 1956, Christie also produced six novels under the pseudonym Mary Westmacott—a disguise that held until shortly after the Second World War when, much to her distress, her identity was revealed in the *Sunday Times*. The Westmacott novels are written in the same readable prose as the crime fiction, but their preoccupations are radically different. These are novels that map—in a variety of ways—the loneliness, alienation, and inhibitions of middle-class mid-century English femininity. These are stories about shyness, insecurity, ageing, grief, and redundancy. They feature ordinary women, sometimes dull or unlikeable women, who for some reason do not quite achieve the easy sociability and unthinking conformity demanded of their class. The novels often focus on enforced periods of reflection, and they articulate a need to escape—through suicide or self-destructive behaviour—from the constraints of middle-class mores and gender norms. Significantly, these stories, often mediated by frame narrators or marginal characters who cannot explain the protagonist's behaviour, refuse the comforts of conventional resolution. Perhaps the most successful Westmacott is the clever, unsettling *Absent in the Spring* (1944), a book Christie claims to have written in three intensive days. An exercise in unreliable narration—or perhaps unreliable self-perception—the novel follows the process through which Joan Scudamore's complacency collapses during an unexpected period of isolation. All the signifiers through which she had read her life are suddenly revealed as open to entirely different meanings: success becomes failure, the familiar becomes strange. This uncanny and disturbing novel was, Christie writes, 'the one book that has satisfied me completely'.

The Westmacott novels also offer insight into Christie's understanding of creativity. In *Unfinished Portrait* (1934), for example, the protagonist Celia is a shy, painfully self-conscious, and overly imaginative young woman. Although dedicated to a fantasy of desire and domesticity—the novel offers a disturbing depiction of coercive control—she also, almost by accident, becomes a novelist. She achieves this by writing about the fabulous rather than the real, relying entirely on 'plausible untruth'. 'You can't write lies about something you know', opines her publisher, 'but you'll be able to tell the most splendid lies about something you don't know' (chapter 15). Christie too told splendid lies about something—murder—that she did not know, but the strength of her writing emerges from what was lacking in the work of the insipid Celia: a confident command of the real, whether that be her knowledge of the Middle East or her

1. **Agatha Christie portrait by John Gay.**

remarkable eye for domestic detail. The Westmacott books demonstrate Christie's psychological acuity; her crime novels deploy that acuity in ritualistic form. She was, quite simply, exceptionally good at imagining plausible reasons to kill (Figure 1).

What did she write?

Christie wrote clue-puzzle mysteries, adventure novels, psychological thrillers, spy stories, short stories, poetry, radio dramas, stage plays, and the hard-to-categorize middlebrow romances that appeared under the Westmacott name. In terms of her literary legacy, though, she is best known and most highly regarded as a writer of 'classical' or 'Golden Age' puzzles: books that invite the reader to solve a crime in tandem with—or ahead of—a brilliant but eccentric investigator. This formula, at base, features a skilled detective outsider who enters a contained environment that has been disrupted by crime. The investigator must be distanced in some way from the community, and they will, through close reading of both place and people, make sense of the clues and provide a satisfactory resolution to the problem. Christie's fame primarily resides in the success of her two improbable but ruthless detectives: Hercule Poirot, a Belgian ex-policeman rendered other by age and indisputable foreignness; and Miss Jane Marple, an elderly spinster, excluded from consideration by gender as well as age. Their detective methodologies would differ, but each exemplified the Golden Age ideal of solving crime through brains not brawn.

Clue-puzzle writing flourished in the interwar years, and in studies of the crime genre it is habitually opposed to the other defining formula of the period, 'hard-boiled' private eye fiction. This mode of crime writing, characterized by a noir sensibility, and traditionally associated with writers such as Raymond Chandler and Dashiell Hammett, featured tough-talking blue-collar protagonists, grappling with the endemic criminality of a hostile urban environment. This landscape of corruption and disillusionment became associated with a specifically American mapping of modernity. The clue-puzzle, by contrast, became associated with England, not least because of Chandler's attack on the formula in his essay 'The Simple Art of Murder', first published in 1944. Chandler acknowledges that Americans also wrote 'logic-and-deduction' novels, but claims that this debased form—with its contrived plots, clichéd characters, and insufferable amateur detectives—finds its apotheosis in the old country: 'The English may not always be the best writers in the world, but they are incomparably the best dull writers.' To Chandler, the superiority of the hard-boiled form lies in its embrace of the real, manifest as a 'revolutionary debunking of both the language and material of fiction'. But while his polemic dazzles—'Hammett gave murder back to the kind of people who commit it for reasons, not just to provide a corpse'—it also deceives. British clue-puzzle writing, particularly as practised by Christie, was never as precious, nor as ideologically secure, as Chandler would have us believe. Rather, it too was a distinctively modern formula depicting a world in which, as Alison Light has argued, 'nothing is sacred'. These were novels built upon the disruption of norms, designed to reveal the corruption at the heart of respectability.

Whatever the rights and wrongs of the argument, the two formulae have proved remarkably resilient. Hard-boiled private eyes have mutated into maverick policemen who somehow persist within the ranks of the contemporary police procedural, while the clue-puzzle regularly reinvents itself through parody, pastiche, and the discovery of new spaces within which a confined community of suspects can be imagined. Golden Age writing is alive and well in the crime-plagued Midsomer villages, the historical evidence sifting of cold case drama, and the painstaking technological clue-gathering of the CSI franchises. It has equally been rejuvenated in Rian Johnson's box-office hit *Knives Out* (2019), and Richard Osman's bestselling *The Thursday Murder Club* (2020). Osman's novels deftly pay homage to Christie's 'Tuesday Night Club', the meetings of which structure *The Thirteen Problems* (1932), a sequence of tales in which Miss Marple's nephew Raymond West, a clever modern writer, gathers his friends—and, of course, his aunt Jane—to tackle unsolved mysteries. Unsurprisingly, on each occasion, it is Miss Marple who triumphs.

Although classical clue-puzzle writing has never gone away, it is nonetheless acknowledged to have had a 'Golden Age', usually regarded as running from the aftermath of the First World War to the beginning of the Second. The formula's dominance in this period has been seen as a legacy of conflict, its light-hearted, relatively bloodless narratives ideally suited to the needs of a traumatized culture. Light again provides a succinct encapsulation: this was 'a literature of convalescence', domestic in orientation and clearly distinct from the imperial heroism of Victorian and Edwardian Britain. Much like the contemporary vogue for brain teasers and crossword puzzles, detective fiction offered a compelling distraction from loss, grief, and the challenges of the postwar world. It also offered readers a different sort of challenge: to solve a murder before the solution was revealed. To enable this, books were supposed to 'play fair', providing access to all the necessary clues, and abiding by the 'regulations' of the genre. In 1928, the priest, biblical scholar, and occasional crime novelist Ronald Knox produced a not-entirely serious 'decalogue', demanding—amongst other things—that there must be no supernatural agencies and not more than one secret passage per novel. Equally importantly, the detective must not commit the crime. The American novelist S. S. Van Dine went further, generating 20 rules that included vetoes on professional criminals, long descriptive passages, and love interests. By way of essential components, he insisted that the detective story must use rational deduction and have a corpse. If a reader is going to invest in a whole novel, he argued, 'no lesser crime than murder will suffice'.

The tongue-in-cheek style in which these 'commandments' were written did more to demonstrate the playfulness of the genre than police its boundaries, and most writers cheerfully ignored such constraints. Indeed, the rules were broken pretty much as soon as they were formulated, with Christie one of the earliest transgressors in the novel that made her name, *The Murder of Roger Ackroyd* (1926). Dorothy L. Sayers similarly broke ranks, in spite of herself having written firmly on the subject of what was permissible within the bounds of crime narrative. It was, she suggested, wholly unacceptable for a detective to fall in love, shortly before publishing *Strong Poison* (1930), in which her detective, Lord Peter Wimsey, does just that. It was, though, the less well known but successful and prolific Gladys Mitchell who most spectacularly threw out the rule book in her debut novel, *Speedy Death* (1929). With an elderly woman detective who is no Miss Marple—indeed, she is a multiply married professional psychologist with a striking resemblance to a pterodactyl—the book breaks a plethora of rules. Such disruptive fictions are important examples of the elasticity and self-consciousness that characterized the genre almost from its inception; but, for all the playfulness that pervades Golden Age fiction, the belief that these books should at least offer the reader the possibility of providing their own solution remained strong.

Beyond the ideal of fair play, the genre's appeal was initially attributed to a range of features from addiction to absolution. These factors were integral to W. H. Auden's influential account, 'The Guilty Vicarage' (1948), which strips the formula down to a sentence: 'a murder occurs; many are suspected; all but one suspect, who is the murderer, are eliminated; the murderer is arrested or dies'. This resolution is achieved through the magical figure of the detective, 'a genius from outside who removes guilt by giving knowledge of guilt'. Auden is open as to whether the guilt is Christian or Freudian in origin, but the ritual process of catharsis—the restoration of a symbolic Eden—is essential to his schema. The consolation of resolution suggested here is integral to Christie's writing, but whether it manifests with quite the clarity suggested by Auden is debatable. There is, after all, something nihilistic about a formula that depends upon everyone wishing to kill, and the identification of a single criminal scapegoat can only do so much to sweep the threat of violence under the carpet and dispel the sense of cultural ill-will. Nonetheless, Christie's fictions make the effort, usually through the prospect of a marriage between two of the surviving characters. Exactly who might qualify for the reward of marriage is a matter for later discussion, but the structural importance of such unions is embedded in her writing from the outset. *The Mysterious Affair at Styles* (1920) sees Poirot resolve a series of relationship crises, repairing a marriage in meltdown and uniting a new young couple, while Miss Marple's first full outing, *The Murder at the Vicarage* (1930), takes a slightly different approach to the restoration of social stability by reuniting a mother and daughter, and tidying up a non-conforming vicar's wife with the gift of pregnancy. Poirot meanwhile becomes a self-conscious, if improbable, manifestation of Cupid, calling himself 'Papa Poirot', the benign protector of lovers and enabler of romance. In just his second appearance, *Murder on the Links* (1923), he shepherds his hapless sidekick Hastings into a safe romantic resolution and, as the novels progress, he repeatedly offers relationship guidance to troubled young people. Indeed, he proves as adept at detecting the signs of desire as those of criminality, as in *The Murder of Roger Ackroyd*, where he diagnoses love as the guilty secret the tongue-tied Englishman Major Blunt is attempting to hide.

That Poirot should function as a matchmaker, and that the inarticulacy of colonial English masculinity should be a source of comedy, points to another significant dimension of Golden Age writing. Across the interwar years, detectives emerged as the antithesis of traditional heroic norms. They were often eccentric, of necessity outsiders, and they triumphed through a command of detail rather than superior strength. While Dorothy L. Sayers' Lord Peter Wimsey and Margery Allingham's Albert Campion hid their brains behind a façade of superficial idiocy, Christie opted to make her first detective a vain and obsessive Belgian, with an 'egg-shaped' head and 'suspiciously dark moustaches'. Poirot is part and parcel of a rejection of conventional masculine authority, and his investigations are predominantly domestic. He believes in sitting back and thinking, not getting up and going. This is, as many critics have argued, a feminized mode of detection, appropriate both to the fair-play impetus of the formula—solutions do not hang on specialized knowledge—and to Christie's respect for the housewife as a figure with significant social responsibilities. Career women are not absent from Christie's novels, nor are they more than averagely figured as murderers, but there is no doubt that domestic competence ranks highly amongst her virtues. The feminized outsider detective is also an underestimated figure within Christie's work. While Poirot intermittently appears as the respected friend of politicians and royalty, and a man with connections across Europe, he is more often dismissed as too foreign or too old, subject to repeated speculation that he is losing whatever brilliance he once had. Poirot uses this misreading to his advantage, lulling suspects into a false sense of security with his broken English and comic mannerisms, and not least of the pleasures Christie's novels afford is the turning of tables upon a range of arrogant, entitled, and offensive suspects. Miss Marple is equally frequently dismissed. Her lifetime 'hobby' of watching human nature at work is hardly recognized as a viable form of knowledge—until, that is, she apologetically, and with a disarming flusteredness, clinically reveals her deductions.

Alongside the centrality of an outsider detective using accessible methods of deduction, clue-puzzle detection in the interwar years depended on a corpse. As Van Dine observed, nothing else would do. In much Golden Age fiction, the body is a cipher designed to generate a puzzle. It must be complex enough to motivate murder, but not so complex as to prompt emotion, and is predominantly approached with an attitude that verges on the hard-boiled. The dead are seldom mourned; of much greater concern is the impact of their death on the living. In a mantra repeated across Christie's career, Poirot asserts that there are 'more important things than finding the murderer' (*Death in the Clouds*, chapter 15), and his imperative, always, is to protect the innocent. Yet, while novels such as *Five Little Pigs* (1942) and *Ordeal by Innocence* (1958) foreground the psychic damage generated by the shadow of unresolved suspicion, in other novels it is social stigma that represents an existential threat. In a culture in thrall to constructions of middle-class respectability, crime contaminates by association. To be 'mixed up in a murder case' is, for the well-to-do, to risk fatal reputational damage; for the lower middle and working classes, it is a matter of shame and anxiety. In a not untypical paradox, however, Christie's earlier fiction offers a cast of young men and women positively thrilled by the sight of a corpse. Here, in novels such as *The Secret Adversary*, *Murder on the Links*, and *The Secret of Chimneys*, being mixed up in murder means adventure and excitement. Christie, writing across a variety of sub-genres and utilizing strongly contrasting investigative figures, was also writing across a rapidly changing set of cultural and political contexts. What murder meant, and its capacity to shock, is not a constant in her fiction. As will be discussed later, her work was always in dialogue with the zeitgeist.

Irrespective of how thrilled by death the clue-puzzle's cast of characters might be, the pattern of order disrupted and reinstated remains central to the formula. Whether the murder took place in a village, on a boat, or on a train, the detective's responsibility was to restore the social equilibrium. Yet it would be a mistake to assume that this restoration inevitably symbolized conservatism. In these fundamentally middle-class fictions, the puzzle depends upon the killer also being 'one of us': a character with social status and something to lose. In this world, the butler—or any other servant, criminal, racial other, or class outsider—cannot be the guilty party. This structural feature exonerates the usual suspects and exposes instead the dark underside of respectability. The clue-puzzle formula insists that *everyone* should have means, motive, and opportunity—the whole community must have wanted to kill—a formulation that cannot help but suggest that the society ruptured by murder is rather less idyllic than it might first have seemed. This pattern is exemplified in *The Murder at the Vicarage* where the most common response to the murder is 'lucky it was only old Protheroe, whom everyone disliked' (chapter 6). Colonel Protheroe is the perfect Golden Age victim—universally loathed and largely unmourned—and this combination of character and plotting speaks not just to the post-traumatic aftermath of the First World War, but also to a shifting understanding of human nature.

The clue-puzzle formula emerged at the same time as Freud's newly translated ideas were permeating the cultural consciousness.

In the interwar years, popular versions of psychology took hold of the public imagination, mobilizing a new language of neuroses, psychoses, and compulsions that would enrich the landscape of crime narrative. Christie was no exception, and her fiction vividly captures Freud's insistence that we all are murderers, in thought if not in deed. 'What no human soul desires stands in no need of prohibition', argues Freud, and 'if we are to be judged by our unconscious wishful impulses, we ourselves are, like primaeval man, a gang of murderers'. '*Mon cher*', echoes Poirot in 1938, 'there are all sorts of deep instincts in man of which he himself is unaware. The craving for blood—the demands for sacrifice!' (*Hercule Poirot's Christmas*, part 4, II). Yet while the Freudian concept of violent impulses held in check by the fragile veneer of civilization offers one explanatory paradigm, much clue-puzzle fiction is also permeated by pseudo-scientific discourses of eugenics and biological determinism. Characters speculate about strains of weakness, dubious heredity, and madness in the family, and while such nebulous constructions seldom provide the solution to the puzzle—they rather act as 'red herrings', playing on the paranoia of a prejudiced readership—it is another indication of the formula's ability to mediate cultural anxieties. Within Christie's fiction we find articulated a range of fears surrounding race, class, gender roles, and the national body that persisted throughout much of the 20th century.

Christie's crime fiction is characterized, then, by a tension between rupture and resolution, anxiety and reassurance. What forms these forces took changed over the course of her career, and in response to the world around her. With the exception of *Death Comes as the End* (1944), set in ancient Egypt, Christie's fictions are all part of the here and now—and they mutate according to the times. She is not writing historically, nor I would argue, nostalgically, so feels no need directly to address the world within which her characters are operating. Miss Marple may look back from the housing estates of the 1960s to a time of exemplary domestic service, but her point, across all the novels, is that human nature does not change, no matter how it is dressed and how many domestic appliances it possesses. And any sense that Miss Marple might yearn for a lost golden age when servants were plentiful and knew their place must be set against her oft repeated preference for the citizens of a new modernity. As she invites the lively young housewife Cherry Baker—possessor of a full-volume 'stereogram'—to become her housekeeper, Miss Marple proves she is enlivened by youth, not afraid or disturbed by it (*The Mirror Crack'd from Side to Side*, chapter 22). Christie's fictions, then, are contemporary novels, imbued with the attitudes of their day—albeit a day that stretched, disorientatingly, from 1920 to 1975. The result is a body of work characterized by both continuity and change. Christie's use of the formula mutates, and the world she investigates changes. Within this, her detectives offer a comforting familiarity of gesture and phrase, while firmly inhabiting and comfortably tolerating modern times.

Although Christie's crime-writing reputation is most securely associated with the clue-puzzle form, this is far from being the limit of her output. Her second novel, *The Secret Adversary* (1922), was the first in a long line of thrillers featuring plucky young protagonists forced to negotiate perilous circumstances and overcome powerful opponents. Writing in the *Autobiography*, Christie succinctly dissects the structure:

> Thriller plays are usually much alike in plot—all that alters is the Enemy. There is an international gang *à la* Moriarty—provided first by the Germans, the 'Huns' of the first war; then the Communists, who in turn were succeeded by the Fascists. We have the Russians, we have the Chinese, we go back to the international gang again, and the Master Criminal wanting world supremacy is always with us.

This summary is hard to improve upon. It can be seen in action across her career, from the Ruritanian romance of *The Secret of Chimneys* (1925) to the Cold War concerns of *Destination Unknown* (1954) and the youth conspiracy underpinning

Passenger to Frankfurt (1970). These fast-paced narratives more obviously change with the times, and can often seem dated now, but they too were successful and popular. Where Christie undoubtedly innovated within this variant, though, was in the regular use of female agents, generating a range of women caught up in intrigue, showing remarkable initiative and resilience in the face of threat.

Throughout her career, and across all the generic forms she used, Christie generated engaging and complex female characters. She also proved herself exceptionally skilled at writing unreliable male narrators. These facets of her style gesture towards a long-established misapprehension about Christie's work: namely that she generated fiendishly plotted novels inhabited by cardboard characters. As with most generalizations, this struggles to hold. Some of her plots are innovative and satisfying; others tend to creak. Some of her characters are thinly drawn ciphers, others are more nuanced and cleverly drawn, and some stand as early examples of the psychological realism more commonly associated with a later generation of crime writers. Her books are remarkably diverse in tone and mood, mediating cultural change and adapting to changing tastes, while yet somehow remaining comfortingly familiar. In the *Autobiography*, Christie described the successful writer as a 'tradesman in a good honest trade', and her output—as the next chapter explores—reveals, above all, a skilled professional at work.

Chapter 2
Means, motive, and opportunity: Christie's techniques

Christie's writing changes across time, not only in response to the political and cultural mood, but also in terms of formula—indeed, she developed a distinctive late style more akin to the claustrophobic psychology of domestic noir than to the clue-puzzle preoccupations of her earlier work. Yet there are ideas, patterns, and problems that persist across her career, along with preferred modes of mystification and character types. She also makes effective use of catchphrases, which work through repetition to render her fiction reassuringly familiar. Repeated images across her writing similarly enable her to draw her character types with the utmost economy, key words and attitudes encapsulating personality and likely behaviour. Proud defiant women throw their heads back as they speak; old family lawyers are neat, precise, and cautious; 'charming young men' have '*no moral sense*' (*Murder at the Vicarage*, chapter 30). Yet however regularly they are deployed, such signifiers cannot be trusted. Christie's fiction is replete with actors, ensuring that no self-presentation can be taken at face value. The mechanics of her fiction are equally unreliable. Christie makes rules and adopts conventions; she equally takes pleasure in breaking and disrupting them.

'It is the eyes of the mind with which one really sees...': Christie's detectives

Christie created two characters who have achieved global celebrity—Hercule Poirot and Miss Jane Marple. Like Doyle's Sherlock Holmes and Fleming's James Bond, they have become icons, exceeding the textual space of their origins and enjoying a form of stardom. Each has been reinvented to suit the tastes of changing times and contexts; both now have biographies of their own. However, while their celebrity matches those of Holmes and Bond, they could not be more different in terms of knowledge and power. As the quotation above—from *Five Little Pigs* (book II, chapter 2)—suggests, their skill resides not in action, but in a concept of vision. They can see through the façade of middle-class respectability, to that which is dissonant, disturbing, or morally corrupt. As suggested in Chapter 1, they function as outsider agents, ridiculed, doubted, or overlooked, because of age, nationality, appearance, and gender. Their crime solving techniques are grounded in the ordinary, the observation of human nature and domestic detail; in their form and function Christie has, suggests Stephen Knight, shaped 'an imitatable method, not a comforting élite personality' (Figure 2).

Beyond this core accessibility, though, the two detectives differ considerably. Poirot enjoys a hinterland of authority, his status as a former policeman and a private investigator offering him entry to spaces beyond the reach of Miss Marple. He is vain, boastful, and capable of embodying an authority at odds with his appearance. Indeed, he changes his self-presentation, becoming more or less foreign depending on the situation. He can speak perfect English, but frequently does not, especially when attempting to lull English xenophobes into a false sense of security. He is gifted with almost indestructible self-belief—manifest in his many immodest statements of genius—but is content for

"What I like about Agatha Christie is she's so full of surprises. This time, she puts poison in cocoa."

2. Helen E. Hokinson cartoon, *The New Yorker*.

characters to mock him before a final turning of the tables.
Poirot is also notably willing to break the law when he deems
it necessary. He has no qualms about lying, is fond of
eavesdropping, and frequently overlooks 'lesser' crimes—theft,
deceit, adultery—in pursuit of the more serious matter of
murder. Yet even here, Poirot is cautious and morally equivocal.
He insists, always, upon uncovering the truth, but what he does
with that knowledge is frequently more concerned with the
spirit than the letter of the law. His observation, in *Dumb
Witness*, that he prefers 'the life of the innocent to the

conviction of the guilty' (chapter 23) succinctly encapsulates an ethical grey area he is happy to inhabit.

While Poirot enjoys taking the stage at the end of his investigations, Miss Marple is usually flustered—prefacing her solutions with some variation of 'I explain things so badly', before setting off on a perfectly lucid series of deductions. Over the course of her appearances, Miss Marple evolves from a lace-trimmed and placid armchair detective to 'Nemesis', goddess of retribution and powerful moral force. She always believes the worst, and is nearly always vindicated, not least because her knowledge is based on a lifetime spent observing human nature. Over the course of her deceptively sheltered village life she has acquired, by her own confession, a mind like a sink. Yet at the same time as she admits the murky depths of her knowledge, and her ability to think like a killer, she attributes a bracing—if faintly absurd—cultural value to her methodology. Sinks, she notes, 'are necessary domestic equipment and actually very hygienic' (*4.50 from Paddington*, chapter 10).

Counterintuitively, and unlike Poirot, Miss Marple becomes a more active figure as her investigations develop after the Second World War. In spite of regular assertions of her age and fragility, and her claim in *A Caribbean Mystery* that her only 'weapon … was conversation' (chapter 6), we find her exploring housing estates, setting up stings, and faking accidents. When Miss Marple calls for the doctor, it is nearly always a ruse covering her pursuit of information or her need to travel, supposedly for her health. Poirot, by contrast, while not ceasing to disapprove of murder, comes increasingly to suffer from ennui. The later novels find him yearning for intellectual stimulation—debating true crime, rereading detective fiction—and steadily less enthusiastic about moving.

Christie also created other 'detective' figures. The cheerful adventurers Tommy and Tuppence Beresford appear five times, as does the inscrutable Superintendent Battle. Mrs Ariadne Oliver—Christie's parodic presentation of the author as detective—first features in *Cards on the Table* (1936) and turns up with increasing regularity in the later Poirot novels, her enthusiasm for activity, for 'doing something', acting as a counterbalance to Poirot's increasingly chair-based methodology. Short stories feature further recurring characters, two of whom, Parker Pyne and the supernatural Mr Quin, specialize in detecting matters of love. Finally, there are Christie's standalone detective agents, ranging from sparky 'modern' young women, such as Lady Eileen 'Bundle' Brent, protagonist of *The Seven Dials Mystery* (1929), to the whimsical figure of middle-aged civil servant Sir Stafford Nye, at the centre of her final thriller, *Passenger to Frankfurt* (1970).

'The quickness of the hand deceives the eye': Christie's plots

Christie is famed for the ingenuity of her plotting, but to understand how she achieves her effects, it is more useful to think in terms of sleight of hand. As the 'mysterious' Mr Quin explains:

> 'That is everything, is it not? To deceive the eye? Sometimes by the quickness of the hand, sometimes—by other means. There are many devices, the pistol shot, the waving of a red handkerchief, something that seems important, but in reality is not. The eye is diverted from the real business, it is caught by the spectacular action that means nothing—nothing at all.' (*The Mysterious Mr Quin*, chapter 3)

This is, in a nutshell, the methodology that underpins Christie's work. She relies on readers' assumptions and prejudices—their inclination to trust or distrust—and her dialogue-driven stories rattle along at a pace that makes it easy to miss the important information disguised by the waving of a red handkerchief.

The red handkerchief equally covers over gaps in the narrative: strategic omissions disguised by ellipses or euphemism. These are central to the success of the novel that did so much to establish Christie's reputation, *The Murder of Roger Ackroyd*. The book's impact is achieved by pushing against Knox's contention that the detective's sidekick 'must not conceal any thoughts which pass through his mind'. Whether or not Poirot's temporary sidekick, the narrator Dr Sheppard, unfairly conceals his thoughts was much debated on publication, but anyone *re*reading the novel finds a new text that revels in ambiguity. Beyond the key omissions, there are countless speech acts the reader might assume to connote Sheppard's paternalistic concern for others, which—seen from a fresh perspective—appear as the self-protective strategies of an anxious murderer. It is hard to encapsulate the impact of the book without giving away this now quite widely known solution, but for those frustrated by this unwanted knowledge, there is consolation available. Christie's plotting, as indicated earlier, depends upon a surfeit of plausible suspects, and this in turn generates a surplus of possible meanings. '[W]ith each reader mapping his own network of clues', suggests the French critic Pierre Bayard, '*everyone is not reading the same text*' and, to prove his point, he painstakingly deconstructs Christie's novel to reveal that someone else altogether committed the crime. Bayard's book-length investigation, *Who Killed Roger Ackroyd?*, argues that these popular fictions, that might appear conservative and 'readerly'—that is, designed for passive consumption—in fact demand active participation. 'Suspect everyone', counsels Poirot in the much later *Third Girl*, and readers would be wise to heed his advice. For these books to function, everyone must have had motive and opportunity, meaning that *of course* somebody else could plausibly have killed Roger Ackroyd. Bayard brilliantly exposes this fundamental structural (in)stability, and others have followed suit, reinventing the solutions of some of Christie's best-known works.

However, for all Christie's ingenuity, scratch beneath the surface and you will find a fondness for predictable tropes, particularly around acting, doubles, and disguise. The books are replete with characters playing parts, confusing questions of time and place, or wholly inhabiting false identities. *Lord Edgware Dies* (1933), *A Murder is Announced* (1950), *After the Funeral* (1953), and *Dead Man's Folly* (1956), all rely upon impersonations to confuse timelines or enable inheritances. Alternatively, there are physical doubles and interchangeable bodies: the inexperienced Christie resorts to twins in *Murder on the Links*, but later makes more serious use of the difficulty of telling women apart. People see what they expect to see and do not look beneath the superficial signifiers of femininity. In *The Body in the Library* (1942) it takes a woman's eye to read the corpse effectively, while in *Evil Under the Sun* (1940), Poirot's early observations about the standardization of glossy, sunbathing bodies represent an easily overlooked clue in the novel's plotting of murderous impersonation. It is also the case that, in a Christie novel, the dead cannot be relied upon to stay that way. There are disturbing reanimations in *Murder on the Links* and *Murder in Mesopotamia* (1936) and the difficulty characters experience in recognizing husbands, lovers, and family members can be seen as a type of psychic blindness—a state of denial or fantasy effecting a failure to see. While sometimes veering towards the unconvincing, at best these plots signal Christie's modernist engagement with unstable identities, her recognition of a performative world in which 'no one human being knows the full truth about another human being' (*Murder Is Easy*, chapter 10).

Christie was also adept at other forms of misdirection. Across her fictions she disguises the intended victim, and turns quite regularly to the double bluff. John Curran, editor of her writing notebooks, sees this as one of Christie's 'most effective ploys' with its *volte face* structure in which the obvious suspect—seemingly cleared by a rock-solid alibi or an unimpeachable witness—is revealed to have been guilty all along. This can be combined with Christie's enjoyment of theatricality, as in *They Do It With Mirrors* (1952), when a 'fake' crime distracts the book's spectators, and the reader, from the 'real business' being performed elsewhere. Christie also evidently enjoys letting readers confuse themselves through prejudiced assumptions. She was particularly fond of tapping into the xenophobia that characterized much of the 20th century. Foreigners are deployed as red herrings from *Styles* onwards, while comedy is created in *Murder on the Orient Express* by M. Bouc's unshakeable conviction that, since the victim was stabbed, it must be the Italian passenger who is guilty. Finally, another mode of Christie bluff is found in grand conspiracies—real or imagined—that disguise motives and murderers lying closer to home, in the intimacy of family and friends. In so many of Christie's novels, then, the skill lies not in plot innovation, but in how adeptly she disguises familiar solutions. And the disguise works because her characters are more complex than they are given credit for—at least when it comes to the psychology of motivation.

'always suspect bluff genial men': Christie's characters

This statement, from Luke Fitzwilliam's notes in *Murder Is Easy* (chapter 7), is sadly misguided; Giles Reed, in *Sleeping Murder*, is closer to the mark when he asserts 'I don't believe murderers are ever a special type' (chapter 13). Nonetheless, Luke's statement directs us to Christie's undoubted reliance upon 'types': characters quickly sketched through a few recognizable, stereotypical, features. These supposedly two-dimensional figures have long been used against Christie, but such criticism ignores the skill and acute observation that enables them to function. Capturing a character in a few deft lines is not easily done, and making that type resonate with readers requires brief hints of personality to be convincing. In *And Then There Were None*, the vicious self-righteousness of Emily Blunt is swiftly captured in the description of her 'encased in her own armour of virtue' (chapter 7), while the horror of Roger Ackroyd's hypocritical, snobbish sister-in-law is neatly encapsulated by Dr Sheppard's suggestion that she is 'all chains and teeth and bones' (chapter 4). In *Appointment with Death* Christie gives us the self-regarding Lady Westholme, who enters a room 'with the assurance of a transatlantic liner coming into dock'. Miss Amabel Pierce, 'an indeterminate craft', is found bobbing bathetically 'in the liner's wake' (part II, chapter 5). Miss Marple meanwhile captures character through analogy. Inspector Slack, she observes in *The Murder at the Vicarage*, is 'exactly like the young lady in the boot shop who wants to sell you patent leather because she's got it in your size, and doesn't take any notice of the fact that you want brown calf' (chapter 26). In a nutshell, we have a policeman who ignores inconvenient evidence and who—as his name suggests—will always take the path of least resistance.

Christie's types, then, are vivid and often comically drawn. Her world is populated by charming men, inarticulate men, and men with chips on their shoulders; complementing them are competent women, silly women, and women whose sexuality runs the gamut from *femme fatale* to mannish lesbian. Villages always have doctors, solicitors, vicars (usually absent minded), and a full complement of spinsters. Businessmen are habitually self-made and financially adept. They tend to have secretaries, predominantly male, who manage their affairs. Culturally opposed to commerce, we find their opposites: artists, actors, and 'queer' aesthetic types. Other lynchpins include professors, scientists, archaeologists, hypochondriacs, and writers. Housewives are plentiful, and working women appear in a limited range of professions: actresses, artists, models, businesswomen (in fashion or beauty), teachers, nurses, and companions. In the later fiction, student radicals and hippies begin to appear. These figures constitute a pack of cards that Christie shuffles, ensuring that her readers cannot easily predict guilt by background or profession, but they also tell us much about the world in which she wrote. Her feckless young men and bright young women are figures she grew up watching—her brother Monty and sister Madge—and they speak to a generation changed by the socio-political impact of the First

World War. This was an era of cynicism, class fluctuations, and a newly mobile androgynous femininity. This was also, still, the age of empire, and the novels are replete with old colonials and military men, figured variously as lonely prolix bores and inarticulate hyper-masculine figures, ill at ease with modernity and struggling to adapt to domestic middle-class mores.

As the aftermath of the First World War gave way to economic depression and the nervous anticipation of a second global conflict, Christie's types subtly mutated to accommodate. As will be discussed in Chapter 3, her representations of gender and society responded to conflict, even if she seldom directly addressed the new war. In the aftermath, she reflected on the welfare state and the legacy of conflict, suggesting in her rootless, often violent, demobilized men and damaged—sometimes deadly—children, the far-reaching psychological consequences of giving licence to kill. And in her final decades, the form of her fiction changed to admit more digressive reflections on issues of topical and personal concern, from care in the community to the death penalty. But although Christie's characters move with the times, they only move so far, because her fiction asserts time and again that 'people do not change' (*Nemesis*, chapter 18). This belief is central to Miss Marple's detective methodology. She can understand crime and identify criminals because she has seen it all before; every transgression has its analogue in the microcosm of St Mary Mead. Miss Marple assumes that social circumstances, from class to parenting, will intersect with ill-defined conceptions of heredity to generate a limited typology within which the skilled reader can detect both good and evil. And yet, when the process is spelled out, it speaks most clearly to the instability of identity:

'Surely it must be the same,' said Miss Marple, 'The—what one used to call the factors at school—are the same. There's money, and the mutual attraction people of an—er—opposite sex—and there's queerness of course—so many people are a little queer, aren't they?—in fact, most people are when you know them well. And normal people do such astonishing things sometimes, and abnormal people are sometimes so very sane and ordinary. In fact, the only way is to compare people with other people you have known or come across. You'd be surprised if you knew how very few distinct types there are in all. (*Murder at the Vicarage*, chapter 26)

In short, it is as clear as mud. Normal people are abnormal, queer folk are sane and ordinary. There is, as J. C. Bernthal suggests, 'a self-conscious frailty in all [Christie's] identity "types"': these are texts that 'problematize "normality" itself'. Cultural categories cannot contain the peculiarities of the human subject, and the detective can only play snap with a lifetime of interpersonal encounters.

A final reason for the effectiveness of Christie's types is something that plays out not within each book but across her *oeuvre*—namely, the dilemmas she sets these figures and the psychology of choice that ensues. In *Hercule Poirot's Christmas*, the potential guilt of a character is ruled out because she 'has too much irony in her nature' (part 6, VI). This is a rare absolute: nearly all Christie's other types seem capable of choosing or refusing the risk of murder. The challenge is to determine what, to any given individual, is worth the risk. *After the Funeral* is a masterpiece of misdirection in this sense. Here the red handkerchief is an inheritance drama affecting an obnoxious and dysfunctional family; yet the murder itself emerges from a wholly different set of motivations, unsuspected because stemming from the ordinary and overlooked. One character's breaking point is another's unconsidered trifle. Equally, the novels reveal uncannily familiar situations, and their consequences, played out across different texts. The hyper-respectable murderer of *The Moving Finger* would rather be a killer than an adulterer; the successful politician in *Sparkling Cyanide* commits adultery, but draws the line at murder; the husband in *Murder in Mesopotamia* would rather kill his wife than accept her desire for another; by contrast, in *Evil Under the Sun*, the husband of a beautiful woman endlessly attracted to other men proves capable of retaining sympathy for his perversely vulnerable wife. In all these cases, desire presents motive for murder, but the reader seeking short cuts gains nothing from this knowledge. However familiar the tormented lover, the jealous husband, the scheming capitalist, or the greedy offspring might be, they do not necessarily resort to murder. Christie may rely on types, but even types have choices.

'I am rather pleased with myself as a writer': Christie's narrators

Dr Sheppard's conclusion, as he looks back over his carefully crafted account of the murder of Roger Ackroyd, neatly points to the skill with which Christie's first-person narrators simultaneously tell the truth and lead the reader astray. Her career is bookended by two particularly brilliant examples, *The Murder of Roger Ackroyd* (1926) and *Endless Night* (1967), the one narrated by James Sheppard, a respectable middle-aged bachelor doctor, and the other by Michael Rogers, a hungry young drifter pursuing money, love, and the house of his dreams. Christie's ability to inhabit both these psyches, and the skill with which she deploys them, has been lauded by critics. Sheppard and Rogers offer seemingly intimate, open narratives, confiding in the reader and exploiting their trust while cheerfully lying by omission. They also delude themselves: Christie is a committed modernist when it comes to demonstrating the limits of perspective and the human capacity for self-deception.

Beyond these 'spectacular' story-telling performances, first-person narrative features frequently in the Poirot series, where its presence acts as a mediating force controlling and often undermining the little Belgian's authority. Nurse Amy Leatheran, the respectable, insular, and secretly romantic narrator of *Murder in Mesopotamia*, cannot get over the absurdity of Poirot, constantly emphasizing his foreignness and his association with the feminine. Her first impression of him is almost scandalized: 'Of course, I knew he was a foreigner, but I hadn't expected him to be *quite* as foreign as he was, if you know what I mean' (chapter 13). Even as she warms to him, her urge to laugh continues, distancing the reader from a narrative in which Poirot's authority is otherwise seldom questioned. Yet Amy also recognizes the skill with which Poirot teases information from the suspects, and although she disapproves of his showmanship, she does not seriously doubt him. The same cannot be said for Captain Arthur Hastings, Poirot's most familiar sidekick.

Remarkably, and despite regular fictional outings as Poirot's right-hand man, Hastings still repeatedly questions his friend's abilities. Hastings serves multiple functions: by embodying a hyperbolic form of 'old fashioned' English masculinity, he too works to assert the foreignness of Poirot. He is governed by the rules of sporting fair play and is regularly scandalized by the ease with which Poirot lies, as well as his fondness for listening at keyholes. Hastings also, showing the Englishman's customary distrust of intellectual enquiry, yearns to be in a different novel—an adventure story—and his insistence on what Poirot *should* be doing serves to further muddy the waters of the plot. Add to this his incurable romanticism and his chivalrous need to rescue women, whether they need it or not, and his value in creating confusion becomes clear. These traits are all established in *The Mysterious Affair at Styles*, where the hapless narrator falls in love with nearly all the female characters. He is, fundamentally, a comic creation. As a narrator, however, he acts as proxy for the reader, making explicit the possibilities under consideration, which in turn are evaluated and dismissed by Poirot. Hastings matters to Poirot, who notes—in a backhanded compliment—that his friend's capacity to grasp the obvious usefully shows the detective what 'the criminal wishes [him] to believe' (*Lord Edgware Dies*, chapter 14). Intellectually, he is the mirror reflecting Poirot's glory, something recognized by the lonely detective when his friend is not there to be impressed: 'I cannot, truly I cannot, sit in a chair all day reflecting how truly admirable

I am. One needs the human touch. One needs—as they say nowadays—the *stooge*' (*Mrs McGinty's Dead*, chapter 1).

Miss Marple is more commonly subject to third-person narration, allowing Christie to range freely in plot and characterization while also permitting access to Miss Marple's point of view. The inner Marple is predictably sharp, constantly drawing parallels between new acquaintances and old, but she is also irreverent and mischievous, taking pleasure in things done well and devising schemes to outwit dull but well-meaning custodians who consider her too frail to manage by herself. The reader also shares in the secret knowledge of Miss Marple's unsuspected detective authority, pleasurably anticipating the moment when 'Nemesis' will emerge from her fluffy cocoon of wool. A notable exception to this approach is her first full-length adventure, *Murder at the Vicarage*, narrated by the good-natured but unworldly vicar, Leonard Clement. Len is another of Christie's inadvertent deceivers. With a secret fondness for detective stories and a much-younger wife—about whom he is 'quite unclerically crazy' (chapter 32)—Len is an appealing bundle of contradictions. Technically a figure of authority within the village, he is cheerfully ridiculed by his wife and nephew, and his deductions are confounded by Miss Marple's far greater insight into human iniquity. He also succumbs to uncharitable feelings about both parishioners and police that must be forcibly repressed under a veneer of ecclesiastical tolerance. His inner thoughts make entertaining reading, and—as with Hastings—ensure that the reader is kept safely distant from Miss Marple's detective process.

'I *am* the law': Christie and the police

This Old Testament statement comes from Poirot at the conclusion of *Curtain*. In his final case, he sees himself acting as judge and jury, appropriating again the powers he once enjoyed as a young policeman in Belgium. Such reminders of Poirot's original official status crop up intermittently throughout the books, but more often he stresses his unofficial position, and suggests that he acts to supplement rather than supplant the police. Naturally, given his defining vanity, he tends to consider himself a cut above conventional law enforcement, but is far too tactful to say this to the police themselves. He is aware of the delicacies of male pride, flattering his way into acceptance and happy to let a range of pompous and unimaginative policemen take the credit for his deductions (*The Murder of Roger Ackroyd*, chapter 7). Whether or not a policeman listens to Poirot serves as a useful benchmark of his good sense. Yet Poirot's official status is always provisional and strategic, and his willingness to ignore, or even break, the law emerges from a preference for restorative justice: solutions that will support the living rather than necessarily avenging the dead.

Miss Marple, operating at a far greater remove from conventional detective agency, shares Poirot's tactful approach to the police, but also more often asserts her fundamental belief in their competence. 'The police aren't stupid' she observes in *4.50 from Paddington* (chapter 3), and is proven right, as Detective Inspector Craddock later hires her as a 'consultant—on murder!' (chapter 16). Craddock turns out to be the godson of Sir Henry Clithering, an old friend and enabler of Miss Marple, whose village life and distant family relations have left her surprisingly well connected. Experience has taught Sir Henry, formerly commissioner of Scotland Yard, that Miss Marple's judgement is to be respected, but he is not alone. Police grapevines resonate at her name, as in *They Do It With Mirrors*, when Inspector Curry turns, on his colleague's advice, to the innocent-seeming old lady for advice on 'the seamy side of human nature' (chapter 12). In *Sleeping Murder*, she is discovered to be a recognizable celebrity, credited with three chief constables in her pocket, and in *Nemesis*, the last Marple novel to be written, 'Detective Inspector Marple' (chapter 17) is described by the Home Secretary as 'the most frightening woman I ever met' (chapter 23). In the circumstances, it is not quite so surprising that the seemingly marginal Miss Marple always gets heard.

Christie's novels evince far greater respect for the police than the Golden Age stereotype—bumbling policemen overshadowed by inspired amateurs—might suggest. She has, though, very fixed ideas of what police competence might look like. Christie's best officers are predominantly 'wooden', most notably the inscrutable Superintendent Battle, who first appears in *The Secret of Chimneys* (1925). Described as having a face 'so singularly devoid of expression as to be quite remarkable' (chapter 11), Battle pops up like a guilty conscience, startling the characters with his prescience and disguising a surprisingly intuitive detective methodology behind his rigorous formal refusal of emotion (chapter 20). Battle's wooden qualities intensify as his career progresses. By *Cards on the Table* (1936), he is not only 'carved out of wood', he also gives the impression of having been built from the 'timber out of a battleship' (chapter 2). There is comedy in this totemic impassivity, but it is also a synonym for middle-class, specifically British, professionalism. The wooden face gives nothing away, and while we do get glimpses of Battle's emotions in his last appearance—*Towards Zero*—there is safety in this unremarkably solidity. Readers of Christie's *oeuvre* will know that no one should trust a handsome policeman.

'a second murder in a book often cheers things up': Christie's corpses

Hastings' confession, in *The ABC Murders* (chapter 3), emerges from his lack of enthusiasm for the 'tedious' business of unravelling alibis. It is entirely typical of what Poirot calls his 'melodramatic soul', but it also points to the complicated and unstable role played by corpses across Christie's fiction. Writing about Poirot's interwar appeal, Alison Light suggests the novels offer a welcome 'refusal of seriousness' (p. 68). The tragic or disturbing aspects of death are seldom foregrounded, and a rising body count is as much a structural necessity as a matter for grief or concern. Indeed, it is a familiar method of moving the plot along, as the enthusiastic child detective Alexander observes while eagerly anticipating a second corpse in *4.50 from Paddington*. Yet, while a second body certainly ups the pace of the fiction, it also increases the pressure on the detective to solve the crime, not least because committing murder is seen as fundamentally ethically corrupting. As Miss Marple notes in *Nemesis*, killing is addictive: 'one doesn't stop at one murder' (chapter 21). In taking a life a boundary is breached, a Rubicon crossed, something that Christie's more sympathetic killers recognize in themselves. Facing up to their crimes at the end of *Death on the Nile*, the murderer is philosophical: 'it's no use being sentimental. I might do it again...It's so dreadfully easy—killing people' (chapter 29).

Nearly all Christie's fictions have a second death, and often they are gruesome—an increase in gore that seems to speak to the ethical decline that the murderer is undergoing. Initiating corpses may be tidy, bloodless, and well planned, those that follow are not. Louise Leidner in *Murder in Mesopotamia* is killed with a single violent blow to the head; subsidiary victim Miss Johnson dies slowly and horrifically after drinking acid. The 'body in the library' could not be tidier, the book's second corpse is burnt to a crisp. In *They Do It With Mirrors*, the first body is neatly shot, the collateral damage victims have their heads crushed. These bodies, far from cheering things up, rather serve to undermine whatever justification the killer might have had for their original action. Indeed, in *A Pocket Full of Rye* (1953), it is the 'cruel, contemptuous gesture' of putting a clothes peg on the nose of the second murder victim, parlourmaid Gladys Martin, that brings Miss Marple to the murder scene like an 'avenging fury'. The peg is an 'affront to human dignity', and it is this, more than the cold-blooded calculation of financial gain behind the original murder, that renders the killer irredeemably wicked (chapter 13).

The plot value of the second death—cheerful or otherwise—is often linked to another regular phrase within the Christie lexicon: 'I've got to play a lone hand'. This recurring assertion flags multiple narrative possibilities. When uttered by a central character, it is a sign of pluckiness—albeit often combined with stupidity. This type of lone operator will subsequently be kidnapped, assaulted, or otherwise incapacitated: undone by bad luck or their foolish underestimation of the enemy. The 'central' lone operator will be rescued and rewarded, but their 'peripheral' counterparts fare less well. Characters who choose not to confide in Poirot or Marple, hoarding their knowledge and in some cases seeking to manipulate it for gain, usually find themselves co-opted as second bodies. This is the fate of Mrs Upward, who opts to 'play a lone hand' in *Mrs McGinty's Dead* (chapter 14), and the blackmailing Louise Bourget in *Death on the Nile*. In this novel we also see the paradigm flipped, when alcoholic authoress Mrs Otterbourne imagines she can achieve celebrity by telling all. She too is swiftly murdered. Christie recognized that knowledge is power, but in her fiction it also, frequently, turns into poison.

The second body, then, may be gruesome, and it may be ethically troubling, but as Jerry Burton, the fighter pilot narrator of *The Moving Finger*, observes, 'we've all got to die sometime'. Jerry's casual fatalism is typical of a necessarily callous wartime British culture and it comes as he rounds up the debit and credit column for the novel. With two happy couples paired off and a working-class second corpse cheerily dismissed as unworthy of grief—unlike the later Gladys Martin—the book almost coercively performs the clue-puzzle's conventional restoration of order. These romantic resolutions bear closer inspection. Read from a different point of view, *The Moving Finger* turns into a fairy-tale in which the unloved Cinderella daughter of a murderous father finds companionship, self-worth, and romance—albeit after a glamorous makeover. She also gets to play a vital role in the exposure of her criminal parent. This romance pattern is repeated regularly across Christie's fiction.

'Murder, I have often noticed, is a great matchmaker': Christie's lovers

It seems improbable that death should act as an aphrodisiac, but—as Poirot explains to Hastings—the tragedy of murder initiates a 'second drama'. As the customary restraint of British society is ruptured, hitherto unimaginable emotions are exposed and, often with a little help from Poirot, hesitantly articulated. This exchange comes from *The ABC Murders*, where Hastings, as usual, is in the process of falling inappropriately in love; naturally he rejects his friend's analysis, but it is 'Papa Poirot' who knows best. And Poirot is not just the guardian angel of lovers young and old, he also has an uncanny ability to detect desire—usually before the characters themselves are aware of their feelings. Miss Marple shares Poirot's nose for romance, her extensive experience of watching St Mary Mead's courtships and consummations giving her a witch-like ability to foretell relationships (and their often unhappy outcomes). Christie's central detectives are, then, also fairy godparents, blessing appropriate unions and unpicking the mess of ill-advised desire.

But what is an appropriate union in Christie's writing? Two modes of happy heterosexual marriage feature significantly in her early work: the companionate marriage, and what might be called the 'safe haven'. The first option is exemplified by the 'partners in crime' Tommy and Tuppence Beresford. When they join forces as penniless, demobilized First World War veterans, they are chums first and lovers second. Marriage is conceived as a big adventure through which they will both have fun. This does not change. In *By the Pricking of My Thumbs* (1968) they are still having fun together, even if the equality of opportunity the marriage once promised seems to have evaporated. Tommy is involved with the security services; Tuppence is bored rigid at home. She does not stay put, but the trajectory of the Beresford novels reveals that the innovation of the companionate marriage fades across the years of

Christie's writing, its interwar modernity sliding gently into postwar conformity.

The safe haven, by contrast, is from the outset a less equal undertaking, and usually involves an older man taking a headstrong, emancipated, or in some way vulnerable woman under his wing. She will be protected; he will be rejuvenated. The template was set early with Hastings' marriage to the acrobatic 'Cinderella' in *Murder on the Links*, but is also on display in *The Murder of Roger Ackroyd*, where the determined, loyal, but wayward Flora prefers the inarticulate, socially awkward, but sturdy Hector Blunt over the good-looking, age-appropriate, but irresponsible Ralph Paton. This type of union—steadying and repairing—persists throughout Christie's *oeuvre*, perhaps most notably in *Ordeal by Innocence* (1958), which offsets a devastating miscarriage of justice with not one but three concluding unions. The long-repressed desire of an older couple can finally be consummated, setting the past to rest; a rebellious young woman chooses an older man who believed in her innocence, over a young man keen to psychoanalyse her; and a virtuous, steady, mixed-race woman is allowed the prospect of marriage to her troubled adoptive brother who is on the verge of emigrating to Kuwait. This displacement beyond national boundaries enables and makes safe the rare prospect of an interracial union in 1950s fiction.

As this final example suggests, there is also a gender-switched variation of the safe-haven marriage. Christie's novels contain plenty of sensible, capable women willing to provide sanctuary for damaged men. This looks likely to be Lucy Eylesbarrow's fate in *4.50 from Paddington*, and there are more extreme manifestations of coping women and child men in *Hercule Poirot's Christmas* (1938) and *The Hollow* (1946). Yet however the gender dynamic is configured, it is a significant feature of Christie's romances that marriage is represented as a positive female choice. Oppressed companion Cornelia Robson, one of the multiple young lovers required to provide consolation at the end of *Death on the Nile*, prefers the security and purpose offered by a reliable middle-aged German doctor to the more obvious attractions of a firebrand young nobleman. The young man cannot believe it, but Poirot offers a telling rebuttal to his protestations: 'She is a woman of an original mind...It is probably the first time you have met one' (chapter 30). For the most part, then, Christie sees marriage to a well-chosen partner as liberating—a release from the pressures of modernity. The flip side of this liberation, though, is an equal belief in women's attraction to rogues and 'weak' men. When marriages go wrong or are simply underwhelming—as in *After the Funeral*—the novels seem to suggest that women who have made poor choices must nonetheless stick with them.

Across Christie's fiction, a career is almost never preferred to marriage, particularly amongst the young and pretty. Characters, from the sentimental Hastings to the pragmatic Poirot, seem welded to the belief that beautiful young women should have fun, dancing and flirting until the correct mate is selected. Jobs are for the lower middle and working class, plus the occasional gentlewoman fallen on hard times; careers are for the plain and unmarriageable, or for those women with the training to support their husband in his profession. In *Curtain*, the scientifically gifted Judith Hastings' desire for a university education results not in an independent career, but in a post as secretary to a doctor whose research she will wholeheartedly support. Before, in due course, she marries him. Sarah King, in *Appointment with Death*, is a rare woman doctor (nurses are plentiful). She too opts for marriage before the novel's end. The terrifyingly competent Claudia Reece-Holland, one of three girls flat-sharing in *Third Girl* (1966), has graduated from Oxford to become a secretary. Her employer, who cheerfully delegates his work to her, patronizingly condemns himself in the observation that she is 'as good as a man in some ways' (chapter 19). Claudia's fate—marriage or career—remains undetermined at the novel's end, but her small role in the narrative nonetheless speaks to the difficulty of escaping normative assumptions. Christie, like many other popular and middlebrow writers of her generation, cannot help but suggest that women's education is of value only in so far as it makes them better wives, mothers, and assistants within a conventional patriarchal world.

The companionate and safe-harbour modes of marriage that predominantly conclude Christie's clue-puzzle novels take little cognizance of desire. This is largely reserved for the murder plots, shaping the crimes of novels such as *Death on the Nile* and *Murder in Mesopotamia* (1936). Central to these two interwar plots, and to desire plots throughout Christie's career, is a distrust of excess. The murderer in *Nile*, concludes Poirot, loved 'beyond reason and beyond rectitude' (chapter 29), a radically unsafe intensity that results in four deaths, including that of the loved one. Too much love can be as deadly as hatred, and it need not find heteronormative manifestation. The desire for a place—a house, an estate, a teashop, even—can drive characters 'beyond reason', as can the love of mothers for their children. *Dumb Witness* (1937) provides a disturbing example: here the murderer's actions reveal that culturally approved ideals of maternal femininity, taken to excess, become pathological. Equally, in the plotting of the novels, instances abound of love cynically performed, exaggerated, and faked for strategic gain. Poirot and Marple's shared belief that 'it's always the husband' is regularly vindicated and counterbalanced by a fair number of murderous wives. In Christie's world, money always has the potential to trump love.

'Atmosphere is important': Christie's *mise-en-scène*

The idea that a place might be complicit in murder, or that an environment might generate forces beyond rational explanation, fascinates Christie. Her books repeatedly raise the spectre of the irrational: superstition, hauntings, and the uncanny manifestations of doubles, dread, and *déjà vu*. Christie's capacity to render the familiar world of the middle classes strange and disorientating is not simply attributable to murder: her *unheimlich* effects also come from the careful manipulation of an ordinary environment that is, somehow, not quite right. This is what Mrs Dane Calthrop's concern with 'atmosphere' articulates in *The Pale Horse* (1961). In a novel packed with inexplicable phenomena, including three witches who oscillate disturbingly between the mundane, the threatening, and the ridiculous, her emphasis on atmosphere is an attempt to distinguish performative trappings from substantive menace. But the importance of atmosphere is also a clue, and a reminder that, amongst other things, Christie's fiction evinces a considerable fondness for smoke and mirrors.

Christie, like many of her Golden Age contemporaries, exploited the interwar vogue for spiritualism. In the aftermath of the First World War, grieving relatives sought consolation in the belief that loved ones had passed safely into a parallel realm and that communication with their spirits might be possible, albeit only through the agency of a medium. Seances, 'table turning', and related psychic phenomena thus became regular features of crime writing, and the suggestive instability of the uncanny haunts the edges of Christie's output. The ghost story is, then, another genre upon which her writing draws, offering opportunities for open-endedness and the absence of explanation. In the story 'S.O.S', from *The Hound of Death* (1933), it is suggested that the atmosphere of an isolated house—in which a murder had once been committed—is sufficient to activate latent homicidal tendencies in a greedy parent. The space suggests the crime, which is only foiled through the intervention of a stranger seemingly summoned by a daughter's desperate prayer. There is an echo of this spatial contamination in *Curtain*, where Hastings, already subject to pressure from the psychologically manipulative killer, finds himself attributing his torments to 'the atmosphere of Styles itself'. Returning to the house that was the locus of Poirot's first investigation, the potential for *déjà vu* is evident, but Hastings feels that the house itself is homicidally haunted (chapter 12). In *Curtain*, unlike 'S.O.S', such phenomena will find an explanation, but the capacity for characters' judgement to be distorted by superstition and environment offers another dimension to Christie's deceptive plotting.

Haunted houses are one route through which Christie exposes the uncanny, another is psychoanalysis. Christie, like most of the mid-century middle classes, had absorbed a range of Freudian concepts, recognizing the power of the unconscious and deploying the language of neuroses and inhibitions. *Sleeping Murder* neatly condenses these multiple shaping forces. Gwenda, having inadvertently bought the house in which she briefly lived as a child, is troubled by *déjà vu*. She suspects the house may be haunted, and worries that she might be going mad, or becoming 'one of those people who *saw* things' (chapter 2). The prospect of clairvoyance is terrifying, a threat undermining the qualities of cheerful, low-brow ordinariness that are integral to Gwenda's identity. Fortunately, Miss Marple is to hand, with a gloriously prosaic Christie suggestion: if you're suffering from *déjà vu*, perhaps you've been here before? She is, of course, right, but her deductions expose another familiar trope: the social and psychic danger of revisiting the past. '*Bury your dead*!' advises Poirot in *Death on the Nile* (chapter 4), seeking to prevent the disaster he can see unfolding. Knowing the truth of the past may be cathartic and might even be a duty, but obsessing over a past that cannot be changed is damaging and potentially deadly. *Sleeping Murder*, however, ultimately balances the psychoanalytic negotiation of repressed trauma with older animistic notions of 'spirit of place' to suggest that old wounds can be healed. The house in which murder has been committed becomes 'homely' again: it is 'fond of us' (chapter 25), concludes Gwenda, once the exorcism is complete.

In the years after the Second World War, in the final phases of her career, 'atmosphere' also came to connote Christie's growing interest in the meaning of evil, and to represent a step change in her investigative practice. By the 1960s, it is possible to see a new mode of crime writing emerge that is more discursive and meandering, and far more concerned with a form of detective instinct than with the logical business of puzzle solving. Novels such as *At Bertram's Hotel* (1965) and *Hallowe'en Party* (1969) present the reader with long digressions not obviously connected to the plot, but seeming rather to reflect on contemporary preoccupations and the pleasures of memory. From debating care in the community to the Proustian pleasure of a perfect muffin, the books inhabit a milieu as much as prosecute an investigation. But it would be a mistake to dismiss these atmospheric constructions as a sign of waning powers. Rather they speak to Christie's evolving interest in understanding evil through what is now dubbed domestic noir. *A Caribbean Mystery* (1964) and *Third Girl* (1966) both present gaslighting plots, in which women are terrorized and manipulated by murderous men. *Nemesis*, meanwhile, borders on the verge of metanarrative. Miss Marple is given a mission by a dead man to investigate an unspecified crime. Her only clue is herself: she knows that the man who hired her believed she has a *'flair* for evil' (chapter 10). Again, the novel is given to lengthy digressions—on heredity and sexual politics in particular—but the reader must pay attention in order correctly to read the domestic horror at the heart of the story. In this case, it is a garden—that most domestic and beloved of English spaces—that becomes the site of repressed horror, symbolized by Polygonum, a flowering shrub 'which swallows and kills and dries up and gets rid of everything it grows over' (chapter 22). Miss Marple, meanwhile, having completed her mission, succinctly explains the transition in Christie's detective writing: '[i]t wasn't really, you know, logical deduction. It was based on a kind of emotional reaction or susceptibility to—well, I can only call it atmosphere' (chapter 22).

* * *

Christie manipulated the crime genre with skill and her nuanced sense of developments within the formula and beyond worked effectively to keep her readership on board through 50 years of change. Yet she was also an evasive writer who claimed to have no interest in politics and who preferred—at least in the early part of her career—to exploit other people's prejudices rather than reveal her own. Nonetheless, Christie too was susceptible to atmosphere, and politics permeated everything she wrote. In the next chapter, I consider how 20th-century preoccupations shaped Christie's writing.

Chapter 3
Not just escapism? Christie in context

Christie lived, and wrote, through two world wars, a depression, the enfranchisement of women, the rise of fascism, the birth of the welfare state, the emergence of the Cold War, the end of empire, and the swinging sixties. Her fiction inevitably bears the imprint of these social and political transformations, and this chapter will take one decade from Christie's long career—the 1940s—as a case study of the ways in which the tensions, anxieties, and desires of a changing Britain found expression in her novels. In particular, it will explore the impact of war on gender roles and responsibilities.

Christie's politics are not easy to categorize, and critics suggest that her writing reveals both radical and reactionary attitudes. Before the 1940s, this duality generated a conventional but optimistic depiction of gender roles. Modernity was offering new possibilities to women, and marriage was imagined as the beginning rather than the end of a narrative. The companionate unions described in Chapter 2 did not just restore stability, they imagined future possibility. However, as the political climate darkened in the 1930s, there are signs in Christie's work of a shift in attitude towards gender. This is most evident in representations of masculinity. In *Murder in Mesopotamia*, for example, we find Poirot pausing in his concluding revelations to offer unusually explicit advice to the anxious Carl Reiter, who has been the butt of a beautiful woman's cruelty: '*Mon ami*, let this be a lesson to you.

You are a *man*. Behave, then, like a *man*! It is against Nature for a man to grovel' (chapter 27). The novel's headstrong modern young woman will in turn be paired with a strong silent type—a man who will 'keep her in her place' (chapter 29). In *One, Two, Buckle My Shoe* (1940), meanwhile, Poirot himself becomes a more forceful and serious figure, a man with 'half the cabinet in his pocket' ('Fifteen', part II). And he needs this, when it turns out that establishment English masculinity—as manifest in the financial elite—is as susceptible to corruption by power as foreign dictators.

In contrast to Christie's earlier fiction, and her fondness for 'making fun of heroes', these examples suggest that masculinity should be taken seriously, both as a concept in need of defence and as a potentially deadly threat to the social order. They also suggest a natural hierarchy in heterosexual relationships, a belief in a relation of dominance and submission. This is quite a change from the cheerful companionship and romantic comedy that dominated her early fiction, and it is a taste of things to come.

Changing preoccupations, changing style

Christie wrote a phenomenal amount of high-quality work in the 1940s. The year the war broke out, 1939, produced *And Then There Were None* and *Sad Cypress*. Before the decade was out, she had published another six Poirots (five novels and a collection of short stories), two Marples, and a Tommy and Tuppence adventure. She produced four standalone novels, two Mary Westmacotts, and *Come, Tell Me How You Live* (1946), a memoir written under her married name Agatha Christie Mallowan. In addition, in two unpublished novels—*Curtain* and *Sleeping Murder*—that would finally appear in the 1970s, she killed off Poirot and produced a 'final' Marple. Somehow, she also found time to adapt several novels for the stage, and produce a radio play, *Three Blind Mice* (1947), that would later form the basis of *The Mousetrap*.

This is an immense list—and it reveals some curious patterns and emergent trends in Christie's writing. Initially, at the end of the 1930s, as the threat of war turns to reality, well-known figures are mobilized. Poirot counters the threat of supremacist thought in 1940's *One, Two, Buckle My Shoe* (published in America as *The Patriotic Murders*) and Miss Marple is central to *The Body in the Library* (1942), even though the novel only tangentially acknowledges the war. Tommy and Tuppence, meanwhile, go undercover in the spy thriller *N or M?* (1941), a paeon to plucky amateurism that offers a rare direct engagement with the conflict. Written when the threat of Nazi Germany was at its height, it taps into the mood of British propaganda and imagines ordinary people saving the nation in its hour of need. As the decade progresses, however, things start to change. *The Moving Finger* (1943), technically a Marple novel, hardly features her, and after this, she will not reappear until *A Murder is Announced* in 1950. Poirot is a more persistent figure, but he too is frequently relegated to a backseat role. In *Sad Cypress* he does not appear for 100 pages; much the same applies to *The Hollow* (1945). By *Taken at the Flood* (1948), he is closer to bookend than detective. He nods wisely in the opening scene and disappears before a timely late reintroduction.

Throughout her career, Christie chopped and changed between her characters, but there is, in the relative paucity of Poirot and the not yet fully realized coming of Marple, an indication of other preoccupations and a desire to experiment: to explore more freely the ideas unleashed by the pressures of war and its aftermath. This transition also reveals itself in the novels' much longer wait for a corpse. In *The Hollow*, *Sad Cypress*, *Towards Zero*, and *Sparkling Cyanide* narrative complexities and characters are explored well before a body appears, and this holding back of the necessary murder changes the tone of Christie's fiction. This was all too evident to her American agent, Harold Ober, who struggled to place these wartime stories in magazines. Christie had throughout the 1930s made good money from American serial rights. But in the 1940s, Ober increasingly found himself rebuffed, and faced with the demand that Christie get her plots moving more quickly.

There is, then, a structural difference between these wartime productions and such early successes as *The Murder of Roger Ackroyd* and *Murder on the Orient Express*. It is a transition in the balance between plot and character that suggests an intensified interest in the psychology of crime and the troubling implications—rather than the plot benefits—of the Freudian paradigm I invoked in Chapter 1. *Sad Cypress*, *Evil Under the Sun*, and *Curtain* all paraphrase the sentiment that our 'unconscious wishful impulses' make us a 'gang of murderers', and the novels are more concerned with exploring the consequences of these impulses than abiding by the rules of fair play. It is a shift of emphasis that demands a new approach to investigating guilt and restoring the psycho-social equilibrium. *Sad Cypress* illustrates this. The novel is absorbed in the psychology of the central character, Elinor Carlisle, whom we first meet in the dock, on trial for murder; Christie also spends a considerable amount of time exploring the class anxieties of her supposed victim, Mary Gerrard. Driving the novel is the visceral power of desire, and the question of whether it has made a murderer out of Elinor. There seem to be no other significant suspects, and while we might distrust figures on various grounds—exaggerated hostility towards Elinor, familiarity with pharmaceuticals—no one else seems to have a plausible motive. The solution, when it comes, relies on a serial-killing backstory that explains everything but which even the most attentive reader would have struggled to 'detect'.

As this dilution of fair play suggests, Christie's 1940s novels offer different attractions to the reader. These are fictions characterized by an uncanny mood and a sense of tension: suspense becomes as significant as detection. And this is a transition that Christie, with her customary narrative self-consciousness, displays in plain sight. At the beginning of *The Hollow*, the eccentric Lucy Angkatell vaguely recalls having had lunch with Hercule Poirot: 'I don't remember much about it because I never think it's very interesting who killed who. I mean, once they are dead it doesn't seem to matter why, and to make a fuss about it all seems so silly…' (chapter 1). These words are typical of Lucy's ruthlessly pragmatic character, but they also tell us that, after 20 years of purposeful plotting, Christie is spending more time on psychological foreplay, and less on the intricacies of puzzle and resolution. She is moving towards a gothic or a noir sensibility, steeped in psychological confinement, repressed desire, claustrophobia, and paranoia. This transition found form in her style, but it is also revealed in a more sophisticated—and more anxious—engagement with gender.

Gender and nation in the 1940s

Total war is so called because it implicates a whole society, and the Second World War—like the First—had a radical impact on women's lives. The still dominant cultural belief that women were 'naturally' domestic and maternal was overwritten by new narratives of citizenship: women could and would be integral to the war effort. Women were conscripted to the armed forces, to industrial work, and the Land Army; many also became single-parent families for the duration, managing rationing, childcare, and household responsibilities often in addition to war work. As women entered the workforce, they acquired a double burden, expected to behave like men while simultaneously performing all the traditional functions of femininity, not least of which was maintaining morale. 'Beauty is your Duty!' trumpeted advertisers and women's magazines, keen to insist that gender 'normality' would reassert itself as soon as hostilities ended, and the wise woman would be careful not to 'let herself go'.

War also places conflicting demands upon men. The 1940s is a complex period for masculinity because it generates two irreconcilable cultural ideals in a short space of time, and expects men somehow to conform to both of them. In the first part of the decade, the needs of war demand that men be soldiers, sailors, airmen—that they put on a uniform and serve their country—with all that this entails. Men work within structures of authority, they encounter adventure, risk, violence, homosocial group cultures, and the boredom of army routine. They must be military, but at the same time, they must not be too military for fear of resembling the national other of Nazi Germany. It is a delicate balance, demanding what the historian Sonya Rose calls 'temperate masculinity'. Men must be peaceable and yet heroic, uniformed and yet cynical, modestly detached from the patriotic ideals embodied by the uniforms they wore. In the second half of the decade, however, the needs of 'peace' take over and demand that men become what Michal Shapira calls 'domestic citizens', expected to prove their citizenship by 'establishing the correct home and family'. Men were now to be home-loving office workers, embracing wives, children, pipes, and slippers, and rather than being looked after by the army machine, they are expected to look after others. Risk has been replaced by responsibility, and about the only commonality of experience is boredom. And, of course, demobilized men were quite literally sent *home*. Unless fortunate in finding appropriate man-making work they faced being emasculated by domesticity, trapped in close proximity to femininity, that most dangerous of psychic forces. They faced a world in which conventional modes of man-making—adventure, risk, war—had become taboo.

These violent transitions in ideal masculinity—generated by national need—brought about transitions in popular culture, in cinema and fiction. Very few war films were made in the years immediately after 1945. It would take a while before a war-weary population had an appetite for seeing on screen what it had just lived through. And crime narrative too underwent significant change. Most critics see 1939, or 1945, as the end of the 'Golden Age' of clue-puzzle writing, and in the aftermath of the war it was the thriller that enjoyed a resurgence, followed a few years later by the emergence of the police procedural. The postwar thriller was also distinctively 'noir'. Writers such as Dorothy B. Hughes and Patricia Highsmith produced intense, uncomfortable, anxious fictions favouring damaged or criminal protagonists, driven by desire and consumed by distrust. For British writers too, heroes changed. In the bestselling work of Hammond Innes and Alistair MacLean eccentric amateur detectives were replaced by tough men employed in, or seeking, self-evidently masculine work—engineering, air transport, security—and these men were often *underdogs*, displaced, lonely, and wounded, unable to fit into the domestic citizenship advocated by a culture of reconstruction. Rather than identifying a murderer, these men would fight an adversary—human or elemental—in the process revealing resilience, and a healthy appetite for risk. Sometimes they would even find a soul mate and the possibility of social rehabilitation. Predictably, in this period, rather less imaginative effort went into imagining new plots for women. After the abnormal hiatus of war, it was assumed that they would easily revert to their default settings: romance, maternity, family, domesticity.

The 1940s, then, present both men and women with an astonishingly rapid social transition: an abrupt shift from the obligatory communality of total war to the almost equally obligatory isolation of domestic citizenship. Christie did not choose to write about the public side of these transformations; rather, she specialized in the psychic climate of the conflict and its impact on the space of home, and, perhaps for this reason, one of her most powerful engagements with the conflict is the demobilization novel, *Taken at the Flood* (1948). This is a rare example of Christie explicitly dealing with a specific cultural moment, and it effectively captures the dislocation generated by the rapid shift from war to 'peace'. It also subverts convention by making the central character a female veteran returning to the uncanny space of home.

Lynn Marchmont, back from the navy, finds herself bored by the man she left behind, a farmer in a reserved occupation. Against her will she is drawn to a different man, a former commando, who shares her restless dissatisfaction with the denuded postwar world. One man embodies the wartime masculinity of risk, adventure, and violence, now imagined as a threat to society; the other represents security and convention, domestic citizenship, and the life she would have had, had the war not intervened. Can the postwar world go back to 'normal'? The answer, according to *Taken at the Flood*, would seem to be only with great difficulty. Lynn, the veteran, opts for David the commando, but he turns out to be a real rather than an imagined threat to society, which leaves her with the stodgy farmer Rowley Cloade (Christie's names are nearly always pertinent, and this is a singularly appropriate name for an inarticulate man who tills the soil). But Rowley too has changed: he is traumatized by not having been allowed to go to war and being deprived of his 'right' to fight. I will return to how Christie resolves this triangle of impotence, frustrated desire, and postwar redomestication. For now, two key points emerge: first, that Christie vividly depicts the irreconcilable gender pressures of the late 1940s, and second, that she, like many others writing in this period, was acutely aware of the need to repair wounded masculinity. The cultural pressure which saw wartime women encouraged to support male morale at all costs mutated after the war into an imperative to support male social, psychic, and—in some cases—physical rehabilitation. In response to this, Christie's 1940s novels not only undergo a structural transition, they also reimagine the plots of masculinity and offer significantly reconfigured romantic endings.

Towards Zero (1944) and *The Hollow* (1946): two tales of the 1940s

Towards Zero is overseen by Superintendent Battle, a man who appears at the beginning of the book as a benchmark of good sense and appropriate masculinity. He is, as usual, expressionless, his 'face carved out of wood...solid and durable and, in some way, impressive'. He is also, conspicuously, 'not a brilliant man', but rather has 'some other quality, difficult to define, that was nevertheless forceful' (part 1, March 8th). This is a description wholly in alignment with dominant ideals of 1940s Englishness and Second World War propaganda: cleverness, or brilliance, is distrusted; the ordinary is valorized as substantial, authentic, and more likely, in the long run, to win a war. Battle will not appear again until the third part of the book, but his brief appearance establishes an immediate and powerful contrast with one of the novel's central figures. Nevile Strange is both the ideal Englishman and a character who troubles that concept:

> If a man could have been selected from amongst other Englishmen as an example of a lucky man with nothing to wish for, a Selection Committee might well have chosen Nevile Strange. He was a man well known to the British public, a first class tennis player and all-round sportsman...He was scratch at golf, a fine swimmer and had done some good climbs in the Alps. He was thirty-three, had magnificent health, good looks, plenty of money, an extremely beautiful wife whom he had recently married and, to all appearances, no cares or worries. (part 1, April 19th)

Nevile's athletic prowess is such that he hovers on the verge of what is, in constructions of English national identity, that most disturbing—and distrusted—of attributes, brilliance; but he disguises this behind a façade of sportsmanship, and a reputation as an exemplary good loser. His concern to 'do the right thing' and be an upstanding Englishman also seems evident in his marital relations. He worries that he treated Audrey, his first wife, badly, and seems determined to make amends by reinstating cordial relations. There is a comical fairy-tale contrast between the two wives: the rich red tones of the curvaceous Kay are set against Audrey's blonde, grey-eyed, ghostly 'quality of intangibility' (part 1, May 5th). The book takes place in and around the home of Nevile's aunt, Lady Tresillian, who has remained close to Audrey since the divorce, generating a social triangle managed through strategic avoidance: the two wives must never appear in the same space at the same time. Lady Tresillian is therefore somewhat shocked when Nevile insists that they visit simultaneously; it seems unlikely that this situation will end well.

Joining Nevile and his wives for a typically tense and claustrophobic Christie gathering are an assortment of rather less favoured men: a social outsider, a class outsider, and a disabled colonial exile. These are all underdogs, a type which Christie always favoured, but the nature of their disadvantage has changed. Typical early Christie underdogs fall into a pattern illustrated by *The Secret Adversary* (1922) and *Why Didn't They Ask Evans?* (1934). Tommy Beresford is recently demobilized, hard up, and unemployed, but he remains throughout plucky, resourceful, and cheerful; the later Bobby Jones repeats the formula. Demobilized from the navy, he too is unemployed, and the prospect of a job in a garage makes him a grave disappointment to his family. But as the adventure progresses, he also proves resourceful and resilient and, like Tommy, gets the girl in an inverted Cinderella story. These are pleasurable, romantic, companionate fantasies. The multiple underdogs of *Towards Zero*, by comparison, tell a different tale, and take on quite different forms, all of which are linked to national anxieties.

Angus has lost his job for telling truth to power, and from this misfortune has followed the break-up of his marriage, long-term unemployment, physical debility, and despair. He is Britishness betrayed and, exhausted by living, he throws himself off a cliff. Christie's fondness for bathos ensures that he only gets as far as a convenient tree. Also present, but barely tolerated by most of the other characters, is Ted, a man whose main crime and qualification for underdog status is his excessive beauty. He's far too good looking to be wholly English and is constantly rendered suspect by the hints of foreignness, and by extension femininity, that adhere to his exceptional appearance. An Englishman, after all, should be characterized by moderation in all things, including looks. Ted is not a major player in the plot and is treated in the end in the way 'the English' prefer to treat foreigners: he is made the butt of a joke. With all the suspects gathered on a boat, Ted is pushed overboard to see if he can swim. He is, in effect, ducked like a witch, and as he starts to sink, his innocence is proved.

Finally, there is Thomas, a self-described 'dull dog'. Thomas is an exemplary English type, the man of few words: 'He did not speak, for Thomas Royde was a man singularly economical of words. His friends had learned to gauge his reactions correctly from the quality of his silences' (part 1, May 29th). His stereotypical Englishness is reinforced by additional characterization: he is intensely loyal, 'alarmed' by emotional scenes, and fond of Kipling (part 2, I). Thomas bears both physical and metaphorical wounds. Since childhood he has nurtured unrequited love for the pale Audrey and, following a mishap in an earthquake, his arm and shoulder have been partially paralysed. In the earlier *The Moving Finger*, wounded pilot Jerry makes it clear that the English 'dog' does not comfortably display his damaged body—it is a site of embarrassment and discomfort because so painfully *visible* (chapter 1). Dominant masculinity (in this case white, colonial, middle-class Englishness) is characterized above all by its status as an invisible norm: authoritative, unquestioned, unexamined. Wounds—psychic or somatic—fracture the hard shell of masculine control, disrupt the cloak of invisibility, and expose vulnerability. When Thomas finally attempts to articulate his desire for Audrey, what comes out instead is his envy of the novel's ideal man: '[Nevile's] got everything that I haven't. He can play games, and swim and dance, and talk. And I'm a tongue-tied oaf with a crippled arm. He's always been brilliant and successful and I've always been a dull dog' (part 2, VIII).

Thomas is emblematic of a cadre of physically and psychologically wounded men who are both part of the postwar landscape, and a recurrent feature of Christie's 1940s fiction. He needs rehabilitation, and the restoration of male agency. And, ultimately, he is rewarded with exactly that, through a nascent romantic relationship not with Audrey, but with a character who embodies another important mode of masculinity evident in Christie's fiction of this period: female masculinity. Lady Tresillian is looked after by an impoverished cousin, Mary Aldin:

> You've no idea what horrors most companions are. Futile boring creatures. Driving one mad with their inanity...To have Mary, who is a well-read intelligent woman, is marvellous. She has really a first-class brain—a man's brain. She has read widely and deeply and there is nothing she cannot discuss. And she is as clever domestically as she is intellectually. She runs the house perfectly and keeps the servants happy...(part 2, VI)

Mary thus combines a wide-ranging, supple intellect (gendered male) with emotional intelligence (gendered female). Christie is an evasive writer, reluctant to expose her own opinions, but the evidence suggests that she believed in gendered forms of intelligence. A woman can be clever, but in most cases her ability will be of a different order to a man's. When women have 'men's brains', they disrupt conventional categorizations and might be regarded as a threat, but as long as such masculine women are willing to channel their intelligence into a culturally appropriate role, Christie seems to believe that they can be aligned with the demands of the dominant culture. Indeed, in times of national need, such reliable, adaptable women are ideally suited to the task of rehabilitating men. Mary, last seen holding hands with Thomas, will support and reward him, enabling the repair of his wounded heart.

The Hollow reveals a similar reliance on oppositional masculinities that embody postwar anxieties. It is another awkward house party, with cross-currents of desire and a bitter strain of inheritance anxiety in the background. The Hollow is the weekend home of Sir Henry and Lady Lucy Angkatell, but much of the desire of the novel circulates around the question of who will inherit and inhabit Ainswick, the Angkatell family seat. The book's dominant male figure is Dr John Christow, a man described by Poirot as having all the 'intensive' male qualities: 'self-assurance, confidence, virility' (chapter 18) (Figure 3).

Christow is a great man, according to his lover, Henrietta, but as with Nevile's brilliance, this excess is not an unqualified good. His doting wife Gerda has come to worship him as an idol—the sort of love that never goes down well in a Christie novel—and his scientific self-confidence embodies both the threat and the potential of modernity. Christie is uncomfortable with this new technocratic elite, seeing them as a type that is oblivious to 'domestic citizenship' and rides roughshod over the needs of others (chapter 8). This is an example of science focused on knowledge to the exclusion of human good—a topic also vigorously debated in *Curtain* and the later *Destination Unknown* (1954)—and it's hard not to see Christow as an analogue for the intangible terrors of the new atomic age. The threat he represents is all too evident when he meets his antithesis, Edward Angkatell:

> The afternoon sun lighted up the gold of John's hair and the blue of his eyes. So might a Viking look who had just come ashore on a conquering mission. His voice, warm and resonant, charmed the ear, and the magnetism of his whole personality took charge of the scene.
>
> That warmth and that objectiveness did no damage to Lucy. It set off, indeed, that curious elfin elusiveness of her. It was Edward who seemed, suddenly, by contrast with the other man, bloodless—a shadowy figure, stooping a little. (chapter 7)

Christow is not just dominant, he is a psychic vampire who drains Edward on the spot (chapter 14). Edward, by contrast, is quite literally Edwardian. Sepia toned and living in the past, he is a man of leisure and a gentleman (in all senses of the world), the current incumbent and last protector of Ainswick, symbol of paradise lost, the past, comfort, and 'peace'. Edward inhabits a queer temporality—the space of childhood, outside the present and

3. Cover image, *The Hollow*, Pocket Book edition, USA 1948.

discourses of progress, production, and reproduction—but before we accuse Christie of nostalgia for a lost golden age, the book makes it clear that this is not a viable mode of postwar citizenship. Edward, in his own way, is as wounded as the men of *Towards Zero*. Since childhood he has been in unrequited love with his cousin Henrietta and he is unemployed, albeit by choice. Without purpose, he has become meaningless and socially illegible. In Christow's words, 'he's one of those vague indefinite people' (chapter 8), while Henrietta calls him 'nice…[but]…inadequate' (chapter 13). He calls himself 'half-dead' and 'not very real' (chapter 13) and will eventually attempt to kill himself by sticking his head in the gas oven, a mode of suicide the novel has earlier identified as peculiarly feminine.

The Hollow also offers another example of female masculinity. Henrietta is a rare portrait of *independent* female agency (she is not on a trajectory towards marriage or part of a detecting couple), and her qualities are linked to familiar signifiers of masculinity. By profession a sculptor, she has an aptitude for the mechanical, enjoying a rewarding relationship with her car, whose male gender makes it an unashamedly phallic appendage. But more importantly, Henrietta enjoys a masculine relationship to work. In Christie's novels, it is a male privilege to be obsessed with work, and to prioritize it above relationships and quotidian domestic needs. By these criteria, Henrietta is undoubtedly masculine, but she is also possessed of emotional intelligence—a quality that in Christie's work is usually gendered female; indeed, it is one of the reasons, along with his command of domestic detail, that Poirot is so often read as a feminized figure. Henrietta's relationship with John is also unusual. There is heterosexual desire—passion—between them, but also an element of homosociality. Henrietta has learnt enough about John's work to act as an interlocutor; and we see her portrayed as a confidant, a Watson to his scientific Sherlock. There are plenty of working women in Christie's fiction, but most of them are enablers: hyper-competent secretaries or housekeepers, or intelligent wives supporting their husbands' glittering careers. Henrietta is different: she actively prioritizes her work—to the frustration of John, who cannot understand why she won't, at least sometimes, think of him, 'and nothing else' (chapter 5). For her, work is an obsession, and this may be why, having lost her intellectual soul mate John, she continues to turn down Edward. Henrietta does not want 'peace', and she certainly doesn't want domestic citizenship.

The fate of the alpha male and the underdog in *The Hollow* is salutary. John gets murdered, and Edward inherits the earth. Or rather, he inherits Midge, a woman repeatedly described as square, dark, and sturdy, and thus ideally suited to a supportive role. And Edward, drained of his lifeblood by John's vitality and modernity, is much in need of support. His long infatuation with Henrietta means that he has not recognized the steady, Christie-approved love of the humble, practical Midge—at least not until she plucks him from the gas oven, thinking 'What Edward needs is someone to light a fire on his hearth—and *I* am the person to do that' (chapter 28). In terms of how the novel refracts its time, Midge also provides a resonant analogue for the wartime worker. She makes her living as a shop girl, and her desire for the retro-comforts of Ainswick encapsulates a powerful current of postwar emotions: the desire for things to go back to normal, the fetishization of home and privacy. It is her desire to be looked after that will restore Edward's masculine agency. They are a rehabilitative version of Christie's earlier more bouncy companionate couples, and exemplify the postwar ideal.

There are other significant masculinities at play in Christie's 1940s fiction, such as the working-class conservative politicians who feature in *Sparkling Cyanide* and *The Rose and the Yew Tree*, but the delineation of damaged men, such as Angus, Thomas, and Edward, takes us to the nub of how, in the words of Stephen Knight, Christie registers social change through 'disruptions to the normal balance of gender and social power'. War has damaged men, and these anxious figures speak to the period's uncertainty as to what exactly, after six years of total war, might now constitute 'normality'. As the new regime of domestic citizenship begins to take shape, then, Christie's fictions do not just expose and investigate murder, they also expose and seek to repair vulnerable masculinities. And this, in turn, leads to changes of emphasis and ending.

Violent unions: reconstructing the romance plot

Mid-century Christie fictions suggest a fundamental belief in the value of work. It is essential for men, and beneficial for women. Angus without work is suicidal; with work, he is a new man. In this, Christie is absolutely on message with regards to the social norms of British culture. Work became a religion in the postwar period, assumed to cure everything. The way to cope with demobilization was to find a new job. In *Taken at the Flood*, David the dodgy commando cannot be repurposed for peace—he was never reliably going to settle into work—whereas Rowley on his farm is quite literally regrowing the nation. Similarly, men who do not work, or perform it inadequately, are best dispatched to the colonies, as is the fate of Roger in *Crooked House* and Roddy in *Sad Cypress*. But, in Christie's world, you *can* have too much of a good thing, as the work-obsessed almost messianic John Christow demonstrates.

Christie's distrust of excess is a constant throughout her career, but it gets particularly vigorous exercise in the 1940s. Too much work is bad; too much love is bad; too much talking is bad; too much belief is bad: all things are best in moderation. It is not surprising that this faith in moderation should increase in the war years—it is part of the valorization of the ordinary that is central to British propaganda of the period. The sceptical, rational, community vision of 'Millions Like Us' is mobilized against those idealists and believers who think themselves superior and would impose their ideas, or their personalities, on others. In this context, the value of the enduring, the resilient, the forceful—but the definitely *not* brilliant—Superintendent Battle becomes clear. Christie would continue to worry about excess throughout her later writing career, but paradoxically, in the 1940s this insistence on moderation is accompanied by a new and unexpectedly violent emphasis on sexual domination.

I have discussed examples of the rehabilitation of wounded masculinity through companionate union, but these are not the most striking feature of Christie's 1940s 'romantic' endings. Rather, what shocks and surprises readers is the presence of violence, both physical and psychological. Earlier in the chapter, I invoked the love triangle at the heart of *Taken at the Flood*. This is ultimately resolved when plodding farmer Rowley finds a way to articulate both his frustrations and his desire by strangling Lynn. This outburst of violence in turn reignites Lynn's passion for him. He has proved himself a 'real' man, capable of risk and violence: 'When you caught hold of me by the throat and said if I wasn't for you, no one should have me—well—I knew then that I was *your* woman!' (book 2, chapter 17). This hyperbolic ending might seem an aberration in Christie's *oeuvre*, but psychologically it is typical of this period, as the ending of the earlier *Towards Zero* indicates. Here, the too brilliant Englishman has gone mad; the dull dog has found his soul mate; and the dubious semi-foreigner has been conveniently forgotten, if not actually drowned—leaving the newly work-reanimated Angus to claim the virtuous Audrey. So abrupt is this resolution that a special marriage licence is needed:

'A special licence comes expensive. I'll need to go to the Bank first thing to-morrow.'

'I could lend you some money,' murmured Audrey.

'You'll do nothing of the kind. If I marry a woman, I pay for the licence. You understand?'

'You needn't,' said Audrey softly, 'look so stern.'

He said gently as he came towards her:

'Last time I had my hands on you, you felt like a bird—struggling to escape. You'll never escape now…'

She said:

'I shall never want to escape.' (part 4, III)

The imagery disturbingly undercuts Angus's apparent gentleness, and the same pattern of repressed threat also features in the earlier wartime novel *Evil Under the Sun* (1941).

At the centre of *Evil* we find a stolid Englishman, trapped in an inappropriate marriage, and another of Christie's independent career women. Rosamund does not just work in a shop, she owns it, and perhaps for that reason, when she and Ken—her pipe-smoking inarticulate misguidedly romantic Englishman—are united at the novel's end, it is the business that bears the brunt of the violence. Rosamund has been forthright: she has asked for a definite commitment before Ken rushes off to rescue 'some other persecuted female'. To which Ken replies:

'You're going to be the persecuted female this time, Rosamund. You're going to give up that damned dress-making business of yours and we're going to live in the country.'

'Don't you know that I make a very handsome income out of my business? Don't you realize that it's *my* business…and that I'm proud of it! And you've got the damned nerve to come along and say, "Give it all up, dear."'

. . .

'And you think I care enough for you to do it?'

'If you don't,' said Kenneth Marshall, 'you'd be no good to me.'

Rosamund said softly:

'Oh, my dear, I've wanted to live in the country with you all my life. Now—it's going to come true…' (chapter 13, III)

As with *Towards Zero* we have the welcome embrace of captivity and a fantasy of submission. To a contemporary eye, it jars; in wartime it repeats the dominant propaganda discourse aimed at women, 'that love and marriage would follow wartime service and sacrifice'. And, of course, this message is not only aimed at women. Sonya Rose identifies 'a significant public apprehension (at least on the part of some men) that women's wartime responsibilities and opportunities would permanently transform the gender order'. Both men and women, then, are being reassured that femininity is indestructible—even if it must be violently reawoken from its dormant state.

The cultures of rehabilitation, psychic and social, that shaped Britain in the aftermath of the Second World War find form in Christie's work through the repeated depiction of wounded men brought into the safe harbours provided by competent women. These women managers promise either to run the lives of their men or, through reflecting back an appropriate image of masculinity, restore their egos to a state of patriarchal normativity. This is a long way from the Christie who liked 'making fun of heroes' and a significant transition from the companionate couples of her interwar unions. Looking back to *Why Didn't They Ask Evans?* it's hard to see Bobby Jones telling Lady Frankie Derwent she will 'never escape' him. Rather, Christie is deploying—with her typical distance and disguise—exactly the rehabilitative strategies of male thriller writers and popular cinema. She is reinstating at least the illusion of male agency in the face of postwar disorientation, but she is also confronting, somewhat uncomfortably, the transitions in her own writing. As I suggested earlier, Christie in this period experiments with the darker sensibility of domestic noir. She spends more time exploring undercurrents of desire, resentment, and need, and she looks a little more closely at the psychology of failure and pain. And then, it might be argued, she struggles to put it all back in the box. Getting back to 'normal' for Christie—as for pretty much everyone in postwar Britain—was easier said than done, and her fiction of this period reveals much that was unspeakable in the traumatized aftermath of war. There is violence in these texts—sexual violence—implied and enacted. There is also the uncertainty of demobilization; the challenge of reconstruction; deep anxiety regarding the social damage of war; and an inability to reconcile the roles she believed best suited men and women with the acutely observed and contradictory evidence of her own writer's eyes. Christie was exceptionally good at judging the zeitgeist, and adapting her fiction to fit, but nonetheless tensions and contradictions emerge. The contorted endings that proliferate in Christie's 1940s novels suggest that it was not just her readers who needed the comfort of a romantic sticking plaster over the psychosocial wounds of war: Christie the writer needed it too.

Christie would continue worrying about the restoration of gender norms, shepherding lively, assertive women into the safe harbour of marriage, or—as in *They Do It With Mirrors* (1952)—ensuring that those already appropriately married were not tempted to stray. She also continued to offer women as repair kits for damaged masculinity. In a particularly comic encounter in *4.50 from Paddington*, for example, young Alexander diffidently attempts to sell his widowed father—a former fighter pilot who has never quite grown up—to Lucy Eyelesbarrow, who he thinks would be a 'decent sort' as a stepmother (chapter 18). Christie declines to answer the question of whether Lucy will accept Alexander's proposal, although Miss Marple is confident of future wedding bells, and this 1957 novel interestingly gestures towards a new set of socio-cultural anxieties emerging. Lucy is a brilliant Oxford-educated mathematician who decides to make a career out of housekeeping: monetizing and professionalizing women's traditional domestic functions. That she might become an academic is not considered a viable possibility. Is this Christie's realism? Are traditional professions impossible for women in the 1950s? The 21st century's belated recognition of women scientists' uncredited work suggests that Christie might have had a point about the difficulties facing women in the boys' club of academia, and not least of Lucy's considerations in forging her alternative career is a desire for independence. Given that Christie habitually

4. Agatha Christie in the kitchen at Winterbrook House, 1950.

depicts scientists as singularly humourless characters, we might also conclude that Lucy is a character with too much irony—and to Christie's mind, too much good sense—to join their ranks (Figure 4).

4.50 to Paddington is a Marple novel, and in her later fiction Christie turns increasingly to her elderly woman detective as an agent of social restoration. Miss Marple becomes a potent harbinger of justice—a modern Nemesis facing those with the hubris to believe they can take a life—and although her investigations provide answers, the conclusions of the novels are not always entirely reassuring. *At Bertram's Hotel* (1965), for example, can only conclude with the promise of retribution, as within the space of the novel, the sociopathic young killer walks unhindered from the scene of her crimes. Christie in the 1950s and 1960s worries—in her conventional displaced and distanced fashion—about delinquency, the damage war has done to children, the welfare state, the end of empire, class mutability, crime, punishment, education, eugenics, ethics, evil, and inheritance. As ever, she handled these topics from the point of view of white, middle-class, 'common-sense' Englishness. The implications of this will be considered in Chapter 4.

Chapter 4
Criminal opinions? Christie's politics

Writing in 1944, the critic Edmund Wilson asked, 'who cares who killed Roger Ackroyd?', before going on to condemn the reading of detective fiction as 'a kind of vice that, for silliness and minor harmfulness, ranks somewhere between crossword puzzles and smoking'. In recent years, however, Christie has been condemned not for her failures in style, plotting, and characterization, but for her reliance on racist stereotypes, anti-Semitic clichés, xenophobia, and class prejudices. She has also, paradoxically, been commended as a satirist of imperial pretensions, a chronicler of political violence, a queer critic of normativity, and a rare example of a Golden Age writer capable of representing ordinary people. All these readings—both critical and sympathetic—are plausible and this points once again to a fundamental instability in Christie's texts. Her texts are 'open': they permit multiple, conflicting readings. Consequently, it is possible to assert both that there are problematic unexamined norms in Christie's writing—for example, her belief in the basic 'rightness' of a mode of conservative, white, middle-class, anti-intellectual Englishness—and that these attitudes coexist with a desire to disrupt and destabilize such norms. The challenge of reading Christie's attitudes is further complicated by the fact that the knowing deployment of prejudice is an integral part of her plotting. 'Criminal opinions' are used both as a succinct index of personality, and as red herrings designed to play upon her readership's ingrained assumptions.

This mode of misdirection was evident from the outset: German-Jewish refugee Dr Bauerstein looks like a prime candidate for murderer in Christie's first novel, *The Mysterious Affair at Styles* (1920), but turns out only to be guilty of spying—a crime for which Poirot refuses to condemn him: 'He is…a patriot. Think what he stands to lose. I admire the man myself' (chapter 10).

Yet, for all that Poirot admires Dr Bauerstein, it is not difficult to find unsettling evidence of racism, anti-Semitism, and a range of other discomfiting ideas in Christie's texts. The books, for example, regularly mobilize the concept of a criminal 'type' and anxieties about genetic inheritance encapsulated in the concept of 'bad blood'. The deployment of such tropes speaks to the persistence of eugenicist thought throughout the 20th century—manifest as both pseudo-science and social policy—and it gives rise to a familiar duality. On the one hand, Christie uses the spectre of 'mental deficiency', variously formulated, to play upon profound social anxieties amongst her readers; on the other, these very anxieties give rise within the fiction to a range of uncompromising attitudes towards social responsibility, law, and punishment. Trying to 'read' gender and sexuality across her fiction generates similar paradoxes. The dandyish Poirot suggests a rejection of conventional masculine norms; the dismissal of a range of unmanly men and non-conforming women confuses the picture. Even Poirot himself, repository of good sense and defender of youth, struggles to negotiate modern gender roles, defending androgynous modern masculinity at the same time as he—along with Miss Marple and Mrs Oliver—condemns the modern girl for always appearing 'dirty'. Christie worked hard to change with the times, but she did not always succeed.

In theory, then, the novels have the capacity to offend a wide range of readers; that they do not, or that these attitudes are tolerated across Christie's global readership suggests either a broad willingness to accept the historical specificity of her work, or an awareness that such opinions are not necessarily determinants of punishment and reward. Just as it is possible to say that Christie's prejudices are evident and that they reveal a wide range of cultural anxieties, it is also necessary to note that they have little bearing on the structures of guilt and innocence within the fiction. Whatever crimes her racial, sexual, and class outsiders might commit, they are almost never guilty of murder.

Race, empire, and the Arab world

Christie's early thrillers are replete with imperial attitudes and racist stereotypes. In *The Secret of Chimneys* (1925), a derivative Ruritanian romance is underpinned by the casual deployment of anti-Semitic stereotype and a vein of xenophobia better suited to the adventures of 'Bulldog Drummond'. The book is full of comedy foreigners, making extensive play with Slavic and Balkan 'types' (ferociously loyal, but bloodthirsty; figured as children within the larger picture of political development). However, even at this early stage, identity categories prove deceptively difficult to read. This is an early example of a Christie novel that exposes national types as easily faked, particularly amongst an international elite whose life experiences cross boundaries of class and culture. British education is an export, and it produces bicultural hybrid citizens, whose acquired or partial Englishness will greatly improve the stock of even the most eccentric foreign land. In the case of *Chimneys*' Herzoslovakia, it helps that its king in waiting is not only British educated, but also blessed with an English mother.

In her literary biography of Christie, Gillian Gill provides a thoughtful reading of *Chimneys*, noting its debt to P. G. Wodehouse and to Anthony Hope's influential adventure *The Prisoner of Zenda* (1894). Gill celebrates Christie's comic touch in her cast of faded aristocrats and pompous civil servants, but she also takes Christie to task for the 'stupidly unthinking' anti-Semitism found in the depiction of financier Herman Isaacstein. The criticism is wholly justified. However, Gill goes on to set Christie's prejudice in context, and to compare Isaacstein with the portrait of Sebastian Levinne, one of the central characters in the first Mary Westmacott novel, *Giant's Bread* (1930). Sebastian is subject to the same corporeal typing: he is fleshly and yellow, with big protruding ears. He is also far more sane, emotionally mature, and sympathetic than the novel's ostensible protagonist, the solipsistic musical genius Vernon Deyre. Genius here, and throughout Christie's work, will never be a trusted quality, and Vernon manages to hurt all those around him, while failing to recognize his own desires before it is too late. Sebastian meanwhile is represented as loyal, intelligent, charismatic, sensitive, discriminating, and—of course—financially astute. Prejudice permeates this novel, both as subject matter and as inadvertent by-product of conventional representation, but Gill is right to see it as an attempt, however flawed, to challenge conventional categories of social and cultural value. *Giant's Bread* champions avant-garde music and prefers sexually experienced bohemian women to conventional society beauties. It is a middlebrow novel in its melodramatic attempt to grapple with contemporary issues, and it is the work of a woman whose day job—writing popular crime fiction—did not quite provide the space she needed to explore her ideas.

In the clue-puzzle crime fiction, Christie's anti-Semitism is less overt but nonetheless persistent, cropping up in the descriptions of minor characters and in casual conversations. In *The Murder of Roger Ackroyd*, stereotypes of Jewish greed and Scottish parsimony are casually conflated when the unpleasant and debt-ridden Mrs Ackroyd is pursued by two 'Scottish Gentlemen' with a 'Semitic strain in their ancestry' (chapter 14), while in *Peril at End House* (1932), Nick Buckley describes her friend Jim Lazarus as 'a Jew, of course, but a frightfully decent one' (chapter 3). In these examples, it is the characters who hold the opinions, but not all such instances can be put down to the prejudices of conspicuously obnoxious, or murderous, figures. The description of Midge's employer in *The Hollow*—a post-Second World War novel—as a 'vitriolic little Jewess' (chapter 14) is both a matter of gratuitous characterization and an opinion casually expressed by a sympathetic character. It generated multiple complaints to Christie's American publishers. Yet Christie was aware of the realities of anti-Semitism. Her autobiography describes a rude awakening when, in the early 1930s, she met the German director of antiquities in Iraq, who revealed himself wholly supportive of the Nazi agenda. His words horrified her, but there is little evidence that she connected this with her own characterological assumptions. This suggests a not atypical ideological dissonance: the political abhorrence of anti-Semitism coexisting with ongoing unexamined prejudice. George Orwell, writing in 1945, neatly encapsulates the peculiar quality of British prejudice when he observes that anti-Semitism, while widespread, is nonetheless not quite 'respectable'. Instead, irrational beliefs find grumbling expression alongside energetic denials: the mid-century British are, for the most part, too hypocritical to be *crudely* racist.

Christie's ingrained assumptions continued to surface, but the early excesses of *Chimneys* were never repeated. Jewish characters, from the 1930s onwards, while still stereotyped as financially canny, appear as love interests and repositories of culturally valued traits (see *Three Act Tragedy* and *Peril at End House*): indeed, some of Christie's fleshy financiers can be found in the backrooms of government, defending democracy and British ideals. At the end of her final thriller, *Passenger to Frankfurt* (1970), the duty of embodying a very national concept of common sense falls to the enigmatic Mr Robinson, a figure repeatedly characterized as yellow-faced and foreign looking. Robinson's ethnicity is never made clear. One character speculates that he might be 'Asiatic', but his association with money, along with Christie's uncomfortable tendency to describe Jewish characters as yellow, most likely makes him a Jew. In *Frankfurt*, he appears as both the power behind the throne of government and the epitome of the middle classes, occupying a stockbroker Tudor house remarkable only for its comfort. He may not escape Christie's lazy physical typing, but no one makes fun of him as they did his precursor, Isaacstein. For Christie, by the end of her career, good financial sense and an adherence to a certain set of distinctively 'British' values is more than enough to make outsiders insiders. *Chimneys'* early prejudices, then, look like ill-judged humour and the youthful adoption of conventional rhetoric: Christie had a chameleon habit of picking up the idiom of the moment, and the book replicates stereotypes that were typical of 1920s popular fiction. However, while there is clear evidence of a change in attitude towards Jewish characters and stylistic progress away from the glib flippancy of 'bright young things', it is hard to find an explanation for the conclusion of *Destination Unknown* (1954). Here the mature and experienced Christie imagines that she can rescue her heroine by having an American secret agent use a blackface disguise. For the modern reader it is a moment of excruciating discomfort, and it reveals Christie as a writer quite painfully of her time.

On a superficial reading, Christie might also be accused of being 'of her time' in her depiction of the Arab world, but here the picture is more complex. Christie had first-hand knowledge of the Middle East, frequently joining her husband, the archaeologist Max Mallowan, on his expeditions. Her travelogue *Come, Tell Me How You Live* (1946), which recounts a season's digging in Syria in the late 1930s, is warmly appreciative of the hospitality, friendship, and beauty of this other world, even if its description of Arab workers as 'subhuman', childlike, and animal cannot be explained as anything other than imperialist and orientalizing. This duality, which—rather like Christie's anti-Semitism—speaks to the deployment of conventional stereotypes alongside more nuanced cultural engagement, is further complicated by Christie's persistent disruption of the imperial position she occupies. Her book, she writes in a preface, is not authoritative. There will be no 'treating of economic problems, no racial reflections, no history'. The book is, she insists, 'small beer...full of everyday doing and happenings'. I will return to the everyday as a means of mediating cultural divisions and reflecting on the instability of Britain's imperial position, but first, a final complication. Whatever Anglophone readers might think of the fiction's orientalizing perspectives, Christie's novels have long been enjoyed—in some cases cherished—by readers across the Middle East.

Nadia Atia discusses the wide circulation of Christie's novels in the Arab world, initially in unauthorized form, but officially translated into Arabic from 1979. She cites the warm admiration of the Palestinian writer Jabra Ibrahim Jabra, who met Christie when he was a young lecturer in Baghdad, and provides a succinct account of the postwar popularity of both Christie and crime fiction in general. Yet in Jabra's account of Christie's writing, it is the puzzle that he praises, seeing the setting as largely irrelevant to the story-driven pleasures of the text. Atia reflects on this, finding much in the fiction to support the argument that Christie's 'Orient' is nothing more than an exotic backdrop peopled by two-dimensional stereotypes. There are ragged natives, unappetizing urchins, comedy travel guides. Yet, like many critics before her, Atia finds such an account ultimately inadequate, concluding that while Christie's descriptions 'conform closely to the expectations of her readership...beneath the veneer of the comfortingly touristic, there are subtle hints that the violence of empire is just beneath the surface'. Christie's Middle Eastern fiction is not simply the closed-environment, clue-puzzle mystery on tour, it is rather a subtle engagement with past history and contemporary politics, mediated through unlikely agents and marginal disruptions.

Christie's writing undermines conventional imperial perspectives by refusing to formulate a clear distinction between civilization and its barbarous other. She is far more interested in points of connection, valorizing what might be termed 'women's time' over the relentless unforgiving march of modernity. In *They Came to Baghdad* (1951), the novel's accidental hero, typist Victoria Jones—a cheerful fantasist and accomplished liar—finds herself caught up in an international conspiracy that seeks to spread misinformation, generate conflict, and ultimately assume power once the world's various warring parties have annihilated each other. For reasons that need not detain us, Victoria finds herself kidnapped, escapes into the arms of sturdy, sharp-witted archaeologist Richard Baker, and, in the midst of the desert, encounters a 'travelling cinema' comprising two men, a magic-lantern-style slide show, and a bench. Victoria watches entranced as she is shown 'the wonders and marvels of antiquity in other lands', and while her pleasure—and Richard's—has an element of paternalism, revelling in the simplicity of the men and their naïve appropriation of Western technology, the encounter prompts a significant dialogue on cultural difference. Richard observes that Arabs find the 'Western impatience for doing things quickly' both inexplicable and discourteous, suggesting they value instead both conversational pleasantries and silence. Victoria imagines that, transposed to a London office, quite a lot of time would be wasted, but Richard's reply dismisses the implicit assumptions behind her response: 'What is time? And what is waste?' (chapter 18). These are vital questions. Victoria will go on to become fascinated by archaeology—both the connection it offers to the past, and its valorization of the everyday and prosaic—and her exposure to other times and cultures will prove integral to the ethics of the plot. This is, argues Judy Suh, a 'celebration of ordinary, workaday domestic life, which is perceived as the basis of a moral recognition of others through time and space'.

They Came to Baghdad imagines the precarious balance of the Cold War world order threatened by a cadre of neofascist *Übermenschen*, 'young Siegfrieds' who will rule over a brave new world (chapter 22). Their representative, Edward Goring, is 'beautiful evil' incarnate—a former RAF pilot corrupted by pride—and a man with an utter disregard for human life. The old and the ordinary must be sacrificed so that the young can inherit. Belatedly understanding the conspiracy and listening with horror as the object of her desire becomes abjectly repulsive, Victoria recognizes her affinity with the forgotten—because ordinary and unremarkable—people of history (chapter 22). Christie's residual orientalism cannot conceive of contemporary Arab characters with whom Victoria might empathize, but she does imagine her forging a connection with the familial, domestic figures of the past, whose mundane lives are being excavated by the archaeological expedition. Recognizing the value of these past lives, she is horrified by Edward's claim that the insignificant bodies of the present simply do not matter.

Reduced to its bare bones, then, *Baghdad* is a surprisingly radical novel. As critics have observed, it up-ends genre conventions by killing off Carmichael—an effective deep-cover spy in the tradition of Kipling's Kim—and instead aligns itself with the comedy of imperial decline found in Graham Greene's jaded, down-at-heel 'entertainments'. Unlike the chameleon Kim, no one mistakes the novel's actual spymaster, Mr Dakin, for a 'native' of any nation other than Britain. Rather they mistake him for a drunk, an Englishman 'gone to seed'. But Christie disrupts Greene's model too, not least by making Dakin's world-saving agents a pair of women. Victoria, and her more professional counterpart, Anna Scheele, defeat the threat of resurgent neofascism with an arsenal of small things: domestic knowledge, family connections, and the skilful deployment of flattery. They succeed by being outside the system, while Edward is ultimately undone by believing in his own irresistibility. That the final clue to the plot's resolution lies with a disreputable piece of knitting speaks to Christie's satirical intent. It also reiterates two of her lifelong preoccupations: the value of domestic knowledge, and the belief, stated plainly in her autobiography, that 'people are the same whatever century they live, or where'. Such a statement, suggesting an unexpectedly psychoanalytic investment in drives and desires that persist across the specificities of cultural and historical difference, is challenging: but it might also be another reason why Christie's writing is able to travel across temporal, cultural, and geographical boundaries closed to more self-consciously 'sophisticated' fictions.

Yet *Baghdad* does not escape its historical moment. The youth conspiracy plot finds resolution through conventionally valorized British national characteristics emerging from the Second World War. The enemy is overwhelming and organized; the British are haphazard—often muddled—but always capable of thinking on their feet. The enemy is intolerant and brutal, the British tolerant and fair; the enemy insists on uniformity, the British accept non-conformity and eccentricity. The enemy has ideologies, the British have common sense. Moderation, conservatism, stability. These values will remain a lodestar for Christie and are reiterated with far greater force in the bizarre 'extravaganza', *Passenger to Frankfurt*. Again, the threat is golden youth, and the 'Young Siegfried' reappears, this time imagined as the focal point of a global conspiracy, the aims of which never become entirely clear. Youth is its vanguard, but as with most of Christie's conspiracies, there are powerful factions pulling strings in the background: the shady representatives of armaments, finance, drugs, and science. The book imagines the collapse of governments across the world, blending historic terrors—a neo-Nazi revival—with new fears ranging from student revolution to anarchy, philosophy, and the decline of deference (chapter 12). The remedy, not yet realized by the novel's close, is a drug that induces benevolence by changing human nature; the main point of view is provided by a man who struggles to take life seriously; the most effective agent fighting the conspiracy is a young woman; the person who knows best, and holds the key to a solution, is an old one. Lady Matilda Cleckheaton, who tries to 'put a little common sense into people's brains' (chapter 20), is the book's repository of cultural values. Outside official structures, rooted in an aristocratic heritage, her social networks save the day.

As the above suggests, *Passenger to Frankfurt* is not an easy book to summarize, nor to categorize as radical, reactionary, or satirical. It functions in many ways as a thought experiment in which Christie asks a series of 'what ifs', while expressing a range of anxious responses to modernity. It is more explicitly political than usual, but the ideas are abstract, and politicians of all stripes are represented as self-serving and ineffectual. Hope lies not in policy, but in the supposedly core British attributes of eccentricity, irony, and imagination. A sanitized mythology of the Second World War underpins the novel, along with a profound belief in the failure of the postwar settlement. It is a conservative vision, but it is not the whole picture of Christie's postwar thought. For all her faith in British middle-class national characteristics, the war does seem to have prompted both concern for the nation and a reconsideration of the social values necessary for it to flourish. This manifests in a reconsideration of which bodies matter. In the first half of her career, she specialized largely but not exclusively in puzzles generated by unmourned corpses; in the second, she turns persistently to moral questions, and pays far greater attention to victims and the demand for justice.

Science, eugenics, and justice

Underpinning Christie's postwar political preoccupations is a growing fear of science and scientists, distrusted not so much for their capacity to destroy the world, as for their clinical willingness to do so. Scientists in Christie's work are seldom absent-minded professors—rather they are characterized as inhuman, cold, and given to extreme ideologies. Their hyper-modern worlds, like those imagined by the indoctrinated young, would have no space for the old, the ugly, and the infirm. Christie was not alone in this fear. Her contemporaries from C. P. Snow to Nigel Balchin to Alistair MacLean depicted abstract scientific thinkers, in particular physicists, as dangerously naïve and lacking in a necessary mode of 'common sense'. Given conventional understandings of common sense as a peculiarly British characteristic, it is but a short step to figurations of the scientist not just as misguided but treacherously foreign. As Christie rather comically puts it in *Destination Unknown* (1954), 'between a first-class tennis player, an operatic prima-donna and a nuclear physicist there is really very little difference as far as emotional instability goes' (chapter 12).

The scientists of *Passenger to Frankfurt* are a little more stable, but they nonetheless reveal the scientific establishment as blithely resistant to thinking about the consequences of its discoveries. Speaking with the air of a 'complacent hardware dealer', Britain's 'top scientist', Professor Eckstein, indicates that he could wipe out half the population of Britain in three days, if desired. His offer declined, he indicates the limits of what science has achieved when it comes to the betterment of the human condition: 'It's not a question of what you *want*, it's a question of what we've *got*. Everything we've got is terrifically lethal' (chapter 14). In Christie's configuration, science is little more than a seedy shop peddling a particularly dangerous form of snake oil. Yet, while Christie seems to recoil from the prospect of a clinical atomic modernity, her fiction persists in asking questions of the dominant discourses of her day. This includes the pseudo-science of eugenics, and her engagement with this—like her rejection of anti-Semitism—is riven with contradictions.

Throughout her career, Christie's writing is permeated with anxieties about heredity and inherited pathologies. In *The Murder of Roger Ackroyd* (1926) more than one character is flawed by a 'strain of weakness', while in *Five Little Pigs* (1942) a woman whose mother has been convicted of murder feels she cannot risk starting a family. In the post-Second World War years, however, Christie's interest in debates around biological and environmental inheritance intensified. It was not just the aftermath of the Holocaust and the dawn of the atomic age that sharpened this focus, but also specifically British debates about education, poverty, and parenting within the welfare state. Intersecting with these questions of social policy were emergent anxieties around immigration and long-held prejudices concerning criminality. As Clare Hanson observes in her study of eugenic debate in postwar Britain, social class, mental deficiency, and criminal pathologies were regularly conflated—with devastating results for those unfortunate enough to be designated defective. In this context, Christie's postwar characters voice anxieties along a spectrum of eugenic, social determinist, and psychiatric beliefs, fears that are both realized and rejected across her plotting. As ever, it is hard, within the fiction, to determine where Christie stands in these debates, but the *Autobiography* offers trenchant support for executing those who kill, not least because she considers this a less cruel punishment than life imprisonment. Significantly, Christie does not confuse class and criminality, but rather turns her attention to those who have had good opportunities but are nonetheless 'tainted with the germs of ruthlessness and hatred'. These people, she concludes, are 'wicked' and might be offered a choice between death and offering themselves up for scientific experimentation. This is one of the more disturbing, unfiltered moments in the late stages of the book. As an intervention, it suggests a degree of tone-deafness, and a failure to recognize that her speculative, provocative consideration of 'restorative justice' sits uneasily within a post-Holocaust world. That her publishers did not object acts as a timely reminder that the reactionary side to Christie was not necessarily out of step with her time.

In contrast to the *Autobiography*, the fiction takes a measured path through contentious debates, providing a nuanced picture of questions that preoccupied British culture. The anxieties cohering around youth, science, and eugenics first find articulation in *Curtain* (written 1940, published 1975). Franklin, the scientist, cheerfully suggests that 80 per cent of the human race could be eliminated (chapter 7), while his assistant, Hastings' daughter Judith, vehemently announces that 'Unfit lives, useless lives—they should be got out of the way...Only people who can make a decent contribution to the community ought to be allowed to live' (chapter 11). Genetic predispositions are also a source of anxiety: in *Curtain*, Boyd Carrington's wife has a 'tainted heritage' she cannot escape, while a child in the later *Crooked House* (1949) is described as being 'born with a kink' (chapter 26). There is some sympathy for this character, but none for the murderer who ends *Mrs McGinty's Dead* (1952) with the despairing cry, 'I'm not responsible. It's in my blood. I can't help it' (chapter 25).

Yet even as Christie mobilizes ideas about good or bad heredity, she sets these alongside environmental factors which are seen to complicate, and in some cases ameliorate, genetic inheritance. She is also quite happy to ignore her own rules. In *Five Little Pigs*, the idea of a murdering mother made marriage impossible; the same applies to a seemingly murderous sibling in *Curtain*; in *Crooked House*, however, a murderer in the family is written off as a genetic abnormality so the novel's narrator can marry the woman he loves. One bad apple does not necessarily spoil the biological stock. Yet this comfort blanket is not offered until after various topical cultural anxieties have been aired. Hanson's observation that postwar society struggled to distinguish between deficiency and criminality is all too evident in *Crooked House*, where the narrator speculates that a boy left mildly impaired by polio might develop pathological tendencies (chapter 23). In *They Do It With Mirrors* (1952), we find Miss Marple weighing into the debate, as she voices explicit scepticism about the value of Lewis Serrocold's schemes for the rehabilitation of delinquents. She, by contrast, believes in a combination of good heredity and hard work (chapter 11). Yet, while this might seem reactionary, the novel's redemptive ending revolves around the marriage of Gina, the daughter of a convicted murderer, who has been adopted and raised as a happy, well-adjusted young woman.

Christie's most substantial discussion of the nature–nurture debate is found in *Ordeal by Innocence* (1958). The plot concerns the murder of Rachel Argyle, the wealthy adoptive mother of five children from disadvantaged homes. Initially it is believed that the guilty party is the most wayward of her children, Jacko. He is described as a born delinquent, someone no amount of good parenting has been able to redeem and, as the novel opens, he has already died in prison. However, as the book proceeds, the stability of these assumptions is steadily eroded. Rachel Argyle, the good mother, is revealed to be hyper-controlling, insisting on shaping every aspect of her children's lives. They nearly all rebel, expressing murderous desires not so much out of bad blood as in response to what a modern young doctor describes as 'smother love' (chapter 9). Equally, the delinquent Jacko turns out to have been speaking the truth: he did not commit the crime. Jacko is nonetheless presented as a criminal on a downwards trajectory, his core criminality repeatedly asserted, possibly to reassure readers disturbed by the vision of an irreparable miscarriage of justice. Christie's books habitually respect the law: here it has failed, albeit in exceptional circumstances (the key witness, after being concussed in a road accident, departs for the South Pole). Yet the reassurance embedded in Jacko's delinquency can only take the reader so far, and the novel cannot help but mobilize the period's most polarizing debates. While Parliament had debated the suspension of the death penalty in the 1930s, public opinion had remained largely supportive of it; however, a series of controversies—including the execution in 1953 of Derek Bentley—gave new impetus to demands for the abolition of capital punishment. In 1957 this resulted in a significant reduction in the number of offences punishable by death, but it would not be until 1965 that abolition was finally achieved. Parenting, and in particular motherhood, were equally hot topics in the period. Postwar pronatalism was supported by new psychological approaches to child rearing, including the widely disseminated and influential arguments of John Bowlby linking maternal deprivation to juvenile delinquency. Yet even as good mothering was considered essential to healthy infant development, too much mothering was seen as inhibiting development, particularly of boys. Appropriate adult masculinity, as many Christie novels suggest, depends upon separation from maternal influence.

The belated exoneration of Jacko opens a can of worms, both for the reader and the rest of the household. In the claustrophobic family investigation that follows, all the siblings are subject to racial and class profiling: Hester, an 'Irish type', is assumed to be self-dramatizing and unstable; Micky, who has clung on to the lost ideal of his golden-haired but gin-soaked working-class mother, is assumed to lack the middle-class quality of restraint;

Mary, the first child to be adopted, is the opposite—criticized as self-contained and selfish, she is presented as having seen her adoption in purely material terms. Tina, a mixed-race child, and the only one uncomplicatedly grateful for the love she has received, is not pathologized as the product of miscegenation, but is rather repeatedly described as inscrutable and 'cat-like'. An otherness adheres to her, even as she is the most dutiful of the siblings. As the novel progresses 'heredity' is discussed from every angle, throwing suspicion onto each sibling in turn; suspicion also—more traditionally—congeals around the father, Leo Argyle, who after years of being ignored by his child-obsessed wife, has found late love with his secretary. Leo's 'hands-off' approach to parenting is presented as preferable to that of the overwhelming Rachel, and his reading of adoption attempts to find a middle ground between nature and nurture, suggesting that blood ties matter, not because of genetics, but because inherited characteristics make children more legible to their parents.

The family structure, then, proposes a familiar Christie trope: too much love is as damaging as too little, whether it be romantic or maternal. The twist, when it comes, is that the obsession with reading heredity has deflected attention from other motives for murder. In the end it is distorted romantic love that is to blame, and the book's eugenic anxieties are proved groundless. Irrespective of the views aired, the assorted adopted working-class offspring have not been pathologically determined by their genetic inheritances. Much of the period's debate around delinquency, deficiency, and meritocracy cohered around the assumed shortcomings of working-class 'stock'. *Ordeal by Innocence*, by contrast, suggests that this stock, transplanted to the privileged soil of the middle classes, is perfectly capable of thriving. Equally central to public discourse was the undesirability of miscegenation, which was—wholly spuriously—seen to threaten genetic stability. *Ordeal*, however, affords relative centrality to an intelligent, sympathetic, mixed-race character who just about survives the text and is offered the prospect of a romantic resolution.

The direct address to class in *Ordeal*, and the book's relatively progressive conclusion, acts as a corrective to the simplifications that dominate an earlier attempt at topicality, *Hickory Dickory Dock* (1955). The novel is set in a London hostel housing an international array of students. These include an American woman on a scholarship; an amiable, deferential, perpetually bewildered African; a serious-minded West Indian woman studying law; a couple of Indians, assorted Europeans, two Englishmen, and, incongruously, a woman who works in a shop. The evident problems with the presentation of Akibombo as stereotypically naïve and childlike have been pointed out by Christopher Prior; he also notes the lesser 'crimes' of which the Black colonial characters are found to be guilty: political agitation, pornography, and communism. None of them, however, are guilty of murder: this is the preserve of white people, and in this case, of privileged white masculinity.

In terms of 'criminal opinions', the exoneration of the book's racial others cuts both ways. On the one hand, Christie studiously avoids demonizing a demographic habitually subject to prejudice and hostility: Akibombo's gentleness undercuts one stereotype of Black masculinity, albeit at the cost of reinforcing another. On the other hand, in accordance with a formula dedicated to the murderous fantasies of the white British middle classes, other races become equivalent to the servant class: not worthy of serious consideration within the puzzle. Irrespective of how Christie may have felt and acted on an individual level, these representations speak to her occupation of what Meta Carstarphen terms a shared 'racist imaginary'. It was an imaginary also inflected by the class assumptions that permeated mid-century culture. In the 1960s, it was still possible to argue that the poor should be deterred from reproducing, and while Christie did not want to sterilize the working classes, she did assume that, for reasons of heredity and environment, they were for the most part suffering from arrested development. Across her fiction, minor working-class characters appear as childlike, immature, and slow thinking. Unless welded to feudal loyalties, they are attracted by easy money, given to hysteria, and they look to adults (the middle classes) to explain difficult decisions: a reliance that proves fatal for the 'greedy and hopeful' Lily Kimble in *Sleeping Murder* (chapter 22). Similarly, the colonial radicals in *Hickory Dickory Dock* are presented as politically immature. When they grow up, they will understand the world through the correct lens of middle-class conservative conformity.

These observations are not intended to condemn Christie. Compared with many of her contemporaries, her fiction is remarkably free of prejudice. She does not demonize racial others, nor assume that the working classes are feckless and dissolute. She does not imagine women are incapable of thought, and—within certain limits—she embraces the queerness of non-conformity. However, as she draws on dominant cultural types to sketch her characters, she replicates many of the assumptions she sees around her. And this leads, particularly in her later writing, to the anxious assertion of disconcerting tropes.

Dirty girls and delinquent boys

It is a feature of Christie's work that her plots repeatedly reveal the instability of the normative family and concepts of respectability. Yet this does not mean that she is necessarily sympathetic to non-conforming characters. Eccentrics and outsiders—sexual, class, racial—are welcome in so far as they conform to the dictates of a specific moral universe. By this logic we can understand both the warmth with which *Appointment with Death* (1950) presents its elderly lesbians Murgatroyd and Hinch, and the condemnation that falls upon a repressed mode of lesbian desire in *Nemesis*. Murgatroyd and Hinch exemplify the ideal of the companionate marriage: they complement each other and are staunch upholders of community ethics. Clotilde Bradbury-Scott's love for her ward Verity Hunt, by contrast, is perverse because possessive, excessive, and controlling.

Nemesis is a late novel, and, like many of the later works, it throws up attitudes and opinions that 'trouble' our belief that we might know Christie as a writer or a person. The book concerns another apparent miscarriage of justice: Michael Rafiel is in prison for a murder he did not commit. However, as he too has been born 'crooked', his past record—including sexual assault—stands against him. In his favour, by contrast, is the fact that the prison governor and his friend Professor Wanstead, an expert on the 'criminal brain', believe he is not the killing type. Halfway through the book, Wanstead provides this backstory for Miss Marple, who has been brought in to search for alternative explanations of the young woman's death. Tackling the question of assault, Wanstead characterizes women as both promiscuous and mendacious. Girls, he suggests, 'are far more ready to be raped nowadays...Their mothers insist, very often, that they should call it rape' (chapter 12). Wanstead is a major figure in the book: Miss Marple's helper and confidant, and his opinions cannot easily be dismissed. Now in her eighth decade, the evidence suggests, Christie is troubled by changing sexual mores, and this conclusion might seem to be confirmed by the indictment of the 'permissive society' as a contributory factor to social breakdown in *Passenger to Frankfurt*. But, as ever, Christie is not wholly predictable. Even in old age, it is difficult to anticipate who her books will valorize and who will be condemned. Indeed, modern youth, with the notable exception of its neofascist manifestations, is more often the subject of sympathy than attack.

Third Girl (1966) is one of Christie's most concerted attempts to depict a new generation, and the plot supplements its familiar dysfunctional family dynamic with a three-woman flat-share and a group of bohemian artists. At its centre is Norma Restarick, who arrives at Hercule Poirot's breakfast table in a curious state of affectless distress. Sporting 'high leather boots, white open-work woollen stockings of doubtful cleanliness, a skimpy skirt, and a long and sloppy pullover of heavy wool' (chapter 1), she is shapeless modern femininity incarnate. Set alongside Norma is the equally modern and gender dissonant masculinity of her delinquent boyfriend, David Baker, whose spectacular appearance will see him dubbed the 'the Peacock' by a mesmerized Mrs Oliver. Together the couple present a perverse inversion of conventional gender norms. Women, once the spectacular sex, have mutated into indistinction (and women's mutability will prove crucial to the plot), while men have become disturbingly 'exotic':

> He was a figure familiar enough to Poirot in different conditions... A representative of the youth of today. He wore a black coat, an elaborate velvet waistcoat, skin tight pants, and rich curls of chestnut hair hung down on his neck. He looked exotic and rather beautiful, and it needed a few moments to be certain of his sex. (chapter 4)

The Peacock's attire evokes the glories of Arthur Seaton's wardrobe in Sillitoe's ground-breaking *Saturday Night and Sunday Morning* (1958), while his attitude is emblematic of the decade's so-called 'decline of deference'; but Christie resists the association with working-class culture, preferring instead to render David safe through comparison with an earlier, more high-status mode of masculine display. He looks, suggests Poirot sympathetically, 'not unlike a Vandyke portrait' (chapter 4). The Peacock thus curiously amalgamates emergent youth culture with an elegant reinstatement of aristocratic masculinity, becoming a new manifestation of Christie's dangerously attractive, ambivalently criminal males.

In actual criminal terms, however, the disruptions of gender are smoke and mirrors: the real criminals are, as usual, those most conspicuously asserting their respectability. Yet even as Norma is revealed to be normal, the book feels the need to tidy up the non-conformity it had briefly presented. The corpse, when it finally comes, is that of the 'poor Peacock', while Norma is rendered ready for marriage. As she reflects on the proposal from the authoritative young doctor into whose arms Poirot has deftly manoeuvred her, she smiles for the first time in the book: 'it was a very nice smile', we are told, 'like a happy young nannie' (chapter 25). Not only has marriage been reinstated as the safest and most attractive option for young women, it has also been configured as a mode of maternal care.

* * *

Towards the end of *A Caribbean Mystery* (1964), Christie gives some telling lines to Evelyn Hillingdon, one of the many strong, sensible women who populate her fictions:

> 'The truth is,' said Evelyn, 'that one doesn't really know anything about anybody.' She added, 'Not even the people who are nearest to you…'
>   'Isn't that going a little too far, Evelyn—exaggerating too much?'
>   'I don't think it is. When you think of people, it is in the image you have made of them for yourself.' (chapter 20)

This warning applies as well to Christie as it does to the characters of her fiction. Anything we think we know about the author, and where she might have stood on the politics and opinions of her very long day, must be recognized—at least in part—as a projection of our own assumptions. Christie, in the end, evades us. This unknowability, a strategic instability that allows her to expose the 'frailty of contemporary normality' while yet keeping her readers onside, is central to her long-lasting appeal, and is one of the factors that has made her work so suitable for adaptation. This longevity, and the proliferations of 'Christies' it has enabled, will be the subject of the final chapter.

Chapter 5
Adaptation and afterlives

Janet Morgan, writing in 1984, describes the immediate aftermath of Christie's death:

> [T]o Rosalind now fell the task of battling to protect the integrity of Agatha's creations: to ensure that Agatha Christie Ltd kept a wholesome distance from proposals for games, strip cartoons, toys, cookery books; and to consider what her mother's wishes would have been with regard to the exploitation of the enormous number of copyrights in every market in the world...

The world has changed, and so has the approach of the Christie estate to their valuable property. There are Poirot jigsaw puzzles, calendars, and spectacle cases, plus mugs commemorating the murder of Roger Ackroyd. Poirot himself has been authorized to continue investigating in a series of books by Sophie Hannah, beginning in 2014 with *The Monogram Murders*, while Miss Marple has been reinvigorated in an entertaining collection of short stories by contemporary writers including Val McDermid, Elly Griffiths, and Dreda Say Mitchell. Beyond these direct reanimations, Christie and her creations have permeated popular culture. In *See How They Run* (2022), a comedy about plans to film *The Mousetrap*—that naturally get derailed by murder—Christie steps in with a well-aimed shovel to save the cast from the killer; in Andrew Wilson's Agatha Christie Mystery Series, the writer becomes a secret agent; in the children's biography picture books 'Little People, Big Dreams' (2016), she becomes an inspirational pioneer woman alongside Frida Kahlo, Maya Angelou, and Marie Curie. She is also the inspiration behind the young adult novel *The Agathas* (2022), in which an unhappy young woman consoles herself with Christie's fiction before becoming a detective herself. An epigraph introduces the writer as 'the bestselling author of all time. Also, one bad bitch.'

As these examples suggest, Christie—as writer, character, and concept—has become a global brand. Her success bridges classes and cultures, defying generational change, and at least some of it can be attributed to the adaptability of her work. Christie's fiction squares the circle of being mutable but recognizable, capable of being reworked while retaining its distinctiveness. This potential was recognized from the outset. In *Agatha Christie on Screen* (2016), Mark Aldridge reveals a history going back to the first decades of her career, with silent film adaptations in the 1920s and a first television appearance for Poirot in 1937, when the medium was in its infancy. Since these early interventions, Poirot, Marple, and the Beresfords have all experienced multiple screen incarnations, few of which bear much resemblance to the characters as created on the page. Margaret Rutherford's Miss Marple is a case in point. Aldridge details how the four films centred around her character, made between 1961 and 1964, moved steadily further from Christie's source material, playing instead to the strengths of Rutherford as a comedy performer. The first film, *Murder She Said*, was loosely based on *4.50 from Paddington*, but the next two films used Poirot novels for their basic plot points. Worse was to come, however, when the fourth film, *Murder Ahoy* (1964), inserted a version of Miss Marple no reader of the novels would recognize into wholly new and largely nonsensical material. Christie was 'greatly distressed', writing that she felt 'sick and ashamed' of the contract she had made with MGM. Fortunately for Christie, the film's poor reviews and Rutherford's advancing age brought the series to an end, but as Aldridge observes, the success of Rutherford in the role—for which she is warmly remembered by many—speaks eloquently to the diversification of Christie audiences, and the extent to which her creations were assuming a life of their own.

The film industry would go on to take Christie's source texts far more seriously, most obviously in the prestige adaptation of *Murder on the Orient Express* (1974), which changed the narrative (and the budget) surrounding Christie on screen. Directed by Sidney Lumet, starring Albert Finney as Poirot, and boasting a cast of A-list actors—Sean Connery, Ingrid Bergman, Lauren Bacall, John Gielgud—it was a lavish example of event cinema that did well with both critics and public. Aldridge summarizes its impact:

> This film saw the transition of Christie from an author whose popular appeal and plotting allowed her works to be deconstructed and reformatted for (normally) low-budget films of middling success to being treated as an author of repute, whose earlier books in particular were now being considered outright classics, rather than entertaining but disposable pieces of popular fiction.

The shift to 'classic' status, and a perception of Christie as a writer enshrining a particular ethos would, a decade later, be reflected in what are probably the best-known television adaptations of her work: the BBC Marple series, staring Joan Hickson (1984–92), and the ITV full-canon Poirot, with David Suchet in the leading role (1988–2013). Both series treat their source material with respect, and both productions cast actors who closely embodied the characters as conceived by Christie. Suchet's Poirot in particular set a benchmark of verisimilitude, offering an intensely precise and mannered manifestation of the character, in marked contrast to the cheerful bon-vivant performance of his predecessor in the role, Peter Ustinov.

Yet, even the most faithful of adaptations cannot escape interpretation and, as the ITV series progressed, so too did the investment in a distinctly Old Testament interpretation of Christie's texts. Suchet's Poirot is pious and devout, and his mission is to confront evil. Ambiguity and accident are thus written out of the stories in favour of clear-cut morality, as for example in the adaptation of *Taken at the Flood* (2006). Here, the plot is altered to replace opportunistic fraud with premeditated mass murder, 13 deaths that give ample scope for the detective's righteous anger. In novels where this kind of clarity simply cannot be achieved, most obviously *Murder on the Orient Express*, Poirot himself must suffer. Christie's original saw Poirot make the calculated offer of two solutions, to be judged by his investigative collaborators, M. Bouc and Dr Constantine. The first is the simple narrative of an unknown enemy who has escaped the train; the second is the truth that implicates all the suspects. As he prepares to give his second account, Poirot counsels Bouc and Constantine 'not to abandon' the first solution 'too abruptly' (part III, chapter 9). He is, in effect, leading his limited jury towards the verdict they will all prefer. The 2010 adaptation, by contrast, imagines a snow-bound exercise in self-flagellation, as an unforgiving Poirot clutches his rosary and walks grimly away from the murderers he has finally, reluctantly, decided to spare. It is a long way from the novel, and perhaps even further from the cross-class champagne ritual that ends the 1974 film, a version of the story that reads Poirot's judgement as something to be celebrated, a final, belated, enactment of justice.

These examples suggest the malleability of Christie's texts: her plots can be altered, her settings changed, her detectives reimagined to suit the needs of new generations, as, for example, in the Japanese anime series *Agatha Christie's Great Detectives Poirot and Marple* (2004–5). This bringing together of the two detective worlds in a single series, bridged by the imagined daughter of Miss Marple's nephew Raymond West, is, however, not the most improbable extrapolation from Christie's texts. That honour goes to the 2021 Swedish TV series *Hjerson*, which gives substance to Ariadne Oliver's much resented Finnish detective.

First appearing alongside his creator in *Cards on the Table* (1936), Sven Hjerson is in total no more than a handful of comedy assertions, but these proved sufficient to generate two series about a queer, grumpy, ice-bathing vegetarian every bit as hostile to publicity as his creator. Christie's Hjerson is the basis of a playful fragmentary metanarrative; that he should come to headline a TV series succinctly suggests the potential of Christie's characterological minimalism.

While Christie screen adaptations now proliferate, during her lifetime she was largely uninterested in their development. When it came to the stage, by contrast, she was actively engaged in translating her work. There is a further contrast in her attitude to the integrity of her fiction. Whereas radical cinema transformations caused her distress, on stage, she was not afraid to make changes, recognizing the different requirements of the form. Most spectacular of these changes was her willing—indeed enthusiastic—culling of Poirot, whose character, she felt, distracted audiences from the drama. Given that the first actor to embody Poirot was the monumental Charles Laughton (in *Alibi*, an adaptation of *The Murder of Roger Ackroyd* by Michael Morton that opened in 1928), it is easy to see Christie's point (Figure 5).

Yet crime thrillers were a hugely popular form of theatre in the interwar years, and Christie had a significant resource at her disposal. Consequently, she too attempted to convert Poirot for the stage. *Black Coffee*, which opened in December 1930, was the first of her plays to be staged. This time Poirot was played by her good friend, the scarcely less substantial Francis L. Sullivan, and the experience seems to have confirmed her first impressions. Christie came to feel that *any* Poirot would complicate the narrative; the audience would 'end up observing the detective' rather than paying attention to what was meant to be observed. As a result of this early discovery, Christie's stage success would have nothing to do with her most famous creations.

5. Charles Laughton, the first screen incarnation of Hercule Poirot.

Christie's theatrical peak was reached in 1954, when she became the first (and, to date, the only) woman to have three plays running in the West End at the same time: *The Mousetrap*, *Witness for the Prosecution*, and *Spider's Web*. Her first major success as a dramatist, however, had come a decade earlier with the adaptation of her 1939 bestseller, *And Then There Were None*. This would go on to become one of the most widely appropriated of her works, and its multiple manifestations offer a compelling snapshot of her global resonance. Since the first UK publication, *And Then There Were None* has appeared under various titles. I will use the current one throughout.

Multi-media Christie

And Then There Were None is a brutal novel. Christie may claim to have written it as an intellectual challenge, and it may throughout retain elements of her customary light comic touch, but the fact remains that she assembles ten more or less unpleasant characters on an island, makes them suffer, then slaughters them in a range of imaginative and often extremely violent ways. The motivation behind this carnage is variously presented as vigilante justice and psychopathy, while the book is thematically preoccupied with hypocrisy, guilt, and the deadly consequences of desire. Through targeted invitation letters, designed to play on the vanities of their recipients, eight strangers arrive on an island where they find a luxurious modern house, two servants, and no sign of their host. Nonetheless, after an excellent dinner, the company are 'satisfied with themselves and with life' (chapter 3). At this point, their complacency is shattered when a recording is played accusing each of them of a crime. They have all got away with murder, and—as rapidly becomes clear with the first two deaths—they are now to face punishment. Cut off from mainland communication, without a boat, and with a storm brewing, there is no prospect of escape from the island: they can only wait, watch, and attempt to detect their adversary. As a fictional entertainment, *And Then There Were None* is astonishingly prescient, foreshadowing the pleasures of the slasher movie, even as it undermines the convention of the victorious 'final girl' (there is a final girl; she does not survive). It is equally embedded in older cultural traditions, drawing on the gothic in its tropes of confinement,

Agatha Christie

paranoia, and an unseen enemy with powers verging on the supernatural, and—in its grisly catalogue of corpses—indulging in the bloody pleasures of Grand Guignol. It is one of Christie's most popular novels, and has been amongst the most widely adapted of her works.

The book's first transformation was for the stage. Frustrated by less-than-satisfactory appropriations of her work, Christie opted to do this herself, and when it transferred to the West End in 1943 her decision was triumphantly vindicated. But the process was not straightforward. On the one hand, the logistics of the plot presented the not inconsiderable challenge of staging the deaths of ten people without descending into farce. On the other hand, the world had changed significantly in the short time since the book's 1939 publication, generating a climate within which the remorselessness of the original book was not certain to translate. Christie dealt with the first problem with typical economy. After the moderately spectacular demise of the first victim, Anthony Marston, poisoned while drinking a toast to crime, most deaths take place in the margins—on balconies, in the dark, off stage—and Christie focuses instead on generating a claustrophobic atmosphere of paranoid mistrust. The second problem required a more radical solution: rewriting the ending to offer redemptive possibility. Christie was not the only dramatist to respond to such imperatives. Terence Rattigan's *Flare Path* (1942), a play about RAF bomber crews and the psychology of wartime survival, was a huge hit with the public, who—unlike the critics—responded enthusiastically to his decision to save a character seemingly destined for death. Equally successful was Noël Coward's *Blithe Spirit* (1941), a love triangle that played death for laughs, and a play that ran for nearly five years. In this context, *And Then There Were None*'s unforgiving conclusion—ten corpses, no survivors, and a suicide's soliloquy on the pleasures of sadism and justice—was not going to work.

Christie resolved the problem by reworking two of the book's central characters, Philip Lombard and Vera Claythorne.

Originally nearly the last to die, they are charismatic figures who—in a different fiction—might have fulfilled the conventional role of the redemptive lovers. It is a sting in the tail of the book that Christie toys with the reader, letting them wonder whether these figures might morally be salvageable, only to reveal them as irredeemable, and as subject as all the other characters to the relentless logic of her plot. Indeed, their moral deficiencies are all the greater for being failures of responsibility: unlike some of those granted an early and relatively painless death—the remorseful General and the guilt-ridden housekeeper Mrs Rogers—they have both failed in a duty of care. Philip has saved himself while leaving 21 African soldiers under his command to die; Vera has let a vulnerable boy drown, knowing that the man she loves will inherit his wealth. The book introduces Lombard as 'a tall man, with a brown face, light eyes set rather close together and an arrogant, almost cruel mouth' (chapter 1). In a book full of animal imagery, he is given 'white pointed teeth' (chapter 3) and figured as a 'panther' (chapter 2). He is also a mercenary, an anti-Semite and a *de facto* white supremacist who believes that 'natives' do not mind dying. Vera, revealing a shared moral deficiency and once again demonstrating her willingness to put desire before sound judgement, later defends him, echoing his callous dismissal: 'they were only natives' (chapter 7).

On the stage, however, Lombard looks subtly different: '*He is an attractive, lean man of thirty-four, well-tanned, with a touch of the adventurer about him*'. This is a benign introduction, and one that draws on the long history of Christie's attractive roguish males. 'Adventurer' is nearly always a positive term in the Christie lexicon and here it works to temper the threatening masculinity of the original Lombard, as does the rewriting of his 'crime': now we learn he was trying to save his men, leaving them food and ammunition while he made a desperate foray in search of help. Later screen versions would consider even this too ambivalent. In the films of 1945 and 1965, Philip Lombard turns out to be someone else altogether—Charles Morley, an inadvertent impostor guilty of nothing but friendship. In the context of the play's debut, however, a willingness to sacrifice himself to save others makes Lombard a British ideal, suitable for wartime and for Vera, who in the stage version is guilty of poor romantic choices, but innocent of child murder. The happy ending, when it comes, fits the mood of the moment but has not aged well. Philip survives because women cannot shoot straight, and the rope which had been awaiting Vera is embraced as the symbolic noose of marriage.

And Then There Were None was a success in both the West End and on Broadway, although—as Julius Green observes—it is not clear that audiences on either side of the Atlantic were watching quite the same play. While Irene Hentschel's London production succeeding in sustaining the tension of the story, Albert de Courville's 1944 Broadway version played much of it for laughs. It would be this version of the story—a 'hilarious chiller thriller'—that would form the basis of René Clair's 1945 Hollywood adaptation. Clair's intent is evident from the opening scene, which takes place at sea. As the boat heaves through the water, the collected unhappy travellers perform comic 'business' with scarves, hats, pipes, and smoke. While each character fulfils the same structural purpose, the casting of major Hollywood player Barry Fitzgerald, as Judge Francis J. Quincannon, turns Wargrave from a pillar of the British establishment—an 'angry tortoise' (chapter 3) with a 'small sour voice' (chapter 9)—into a rather more cheerful embodiment of Irish-American 'hail-fellow-well-met'. Also mutating for the screen, and for comic effect, we find Christie's amoral 'young God' Tony Marston emerging as Prince Nikita Stahlov, a 'professional guest', who will raise a toast to anything in pursuit of a drink. The stately butler Rogers, meanwhile, is liberated. Shedding deference and inhibitions, he proves he is not poisoning the guests by drinking their cocktails. The guests spy on each other through keyholes or, in Emily Brent's case, through binoculars, and playful point of view shots keep the audience at a safe comic distance from identification or distress. Blore and

Armstrong, framed in mid-shot, vigorously debate Rogers's guilt, oblivious to his dead feet sticking out of a bush in the foreground. When the supposedly dead judge is carried out, we watch from the point of view of a cat, which weaves its way through the narrative like a witch's familiar, marking the characters for death before a final proto-Blofeldian appearance, being stroked by Quincannon as he makes his confession (Figure 6).

The overall impact is distinctly jaunty, oscillating between 1930s screwball comedy and 1940s noir, while remaining remarkably faithful to the structure of Christie's play. The film did well at the box office, and its success seems to have encouraged later adaptors to opt for 'repetition with variation' rather than attempting a more 'interpretative act of appropriation'. George Pollock's 1965 version doubles down on a tried and tested formula, changing the scenery, the names, and some of the crimes, but otherwise largely echoing Clair's film in plot, structure, and affect—a process assisted by the

6. *And Then There Were None*, dir. René Clair, 1945.

return of the ubiquitous cat. Here, a cable car takes the eight guests—a cast of British cinema stalwarts, with a sprinkling of European glamour—to a house perched atop a snowy mountain. The changing social mores of the 1960s make themselves felt in a jazzy soundtrack, a pop star, an extravagant fight sequence, and a little more sex, implied if not explicit. Innovation, when it comes, is provided by a 'whodunnit break', activated as Vera and Lombard face up to each other in long shot. Cinema goers were asked to turn to their neighbours and speculate about the solution for a minute before the film resumed. This bizarre interruption aside, the production is derivative but not without a degree of camp pleasure, as for example in Wilfrid Hyde White's delightfully avuncular delivery of the judge's confession: 'I always enjoyed that' he smilingly reminisces of sentencing people to death.

Continuity rather than change also marked the 1974 production, which was produced by the same man, Harry Alan Towers. The law of diminishing returns applies, and neither the dramatic desert landscape nor the presence of heavyweight stars such as Oliver Reed, Charles Aznavour, and Richard Attenborough can redeem a stylized drama that feels much longer than its relatively brisk 98-minute running time. Astonishingly, Towers would go back to the well one more time, producing a safari-set version in 1989 that has—by Aldridge's account—justifiably disappeared from circulation. But while these repetitions were in play in the Anglo-American film industry, far greater innovation was on display elsewhere in the world. The year 1965 also saw the production of *Gumnaam*, a Hindi-language spectacular that introduces criminal conspiracy, undercover police, and dance sequences into the framework of Christie's story, while some 20 years later film makers in the USSR took the radical decision to return to Christie's original ending. This version, from 1987, closely follows the contours of the novel, and offers little relief from the text's most terrifying implications. It would be nearly 30 years before an English-language production would follow this lead, and before then the story would move media again, appearing as a 'point-and-click' video game. *And Then There Were None* (2005) offered the familiar cast of characters and a range of possible endings, and was played from the perspective of a neutral third person invented for the game (Patrick Narracott). Its reception seems to have been lukewarm, but it nonetheless spawned a new Christie 'genre'. At the time of writing, the *Agatha Christie* series—now under the control of French developer Microids—numbers 12 titles, including several Marples, assorted Poirots, and two versions of *Murder on the Orient Express*.

In December 2015, the kaleidoscope shifted again as the BBC launched its three-part prestige adaptation of *And Then There Were None*. Scripted by Sarah Phelps, a writer whose credits ranged from *EastEnders* to Dickens, the production went back to the book in setting, character, and ending. If René Clair's film speaks to war weariness and a consequent desire for light entertainment, Phelps's visceral, blood-soaked adaptation suggests an almost nihilistic mood of social and psychic collapse. From the outset the tone is dark and foreboding: Rogers and his wife greet the travellers looking uncannily like Grant Wood's couple in 'American Gothic', while a degree of paranoia is immediately suggested through Blore taking notes on his companions. Eyeing Lombard, he jots down 'Fenian', succinctly dripping the political anxieties of the period into the mix. Lombard himself has by this time already eyed up Vera on the train. They will go on to 'enjoy' a fevered sexual encounter, but here the scrutiny is predatory, hungry. This Lombard is undoubtedly the 'panther' of Christie's original. Down in the kitchens, meanwhile, the Rogers go about their business, but the *mise-en-scène* is far from domestic. The camera lingers on kitchen weaponry and lumps of offal, while Mrs Rogers chops meat, boils lobsters, and feeds buckets of blood to hungry seagulls. Death could hardly be more clearly foreshadowed, and the murders, when they come, commit to the Grand Guignol aesthetic. The General is not just coshed, his head is smashed; Rogers is not simply killed with an axe, he is disembowelled.

The violence of the adaptation is psychological as well as physical. The class and gender hierarchies of the period emerge in rudeness, rage, and hysterical outbursts; Emily Brent's unforgiving pious hypocrisy is laid bare in a horrific humiliation of Mrs Rogers, and the veneer of civilization crumbles amidst a desperate bacchanal, as the remaining four characters drink, snort coke, and dance in the hope of warding off death. The actors, in turn, give their utmost: from Charles Dance's desiccated judge to Miranda Richardson's vicious Brent to Aiden Turner's dangerously charming Lombard, a piece of casting that benefited from the actor's heroic turn in *Poldark*. Interviewed in 2017, Phelps stressed the cruelty of the novel, seeing it as combining the remorselessness of a Greek tragedy with an acute awareness of contemporary anxieties. Her aim in adapting, she said, was to explore the 'niceties being stripped away', to ask, in effect, 'who we are when the lights go out?' In this, the story of *And Then There Were None* comes full circle, ending where Christie began with atavistic brutality and inescapable retributive justice.

The history of *And Then There Were None* makes the mutability of a Christie story abundantly clear, and this has been integral to her success, and to the extent to which 'Agatha Christie', as brand and concept, has expanded far beyond the woman who wrote novels with professional regularity, loved the theatre, and preferred to be known as a housewife. Yet adaptability alone can only take us so far in understanding her appeal. Her global renown is both a phenomenon and a mystery, and it brings us back to the question with which this short introduction began. Why, of all the popular writers of the 20th century, should it be Christie who achieved so much and left such a remarkable legacy?

Why Christie?

Various answers have been proposed to explain Christie's success. Robert Barnard's early intervention, *A Talent to Deceive*, published just four years after her death, emphasizes the 'wonderful simplicity' of her classic deceptions, a skill that keeps her writing fresh and ensures that readers 'always want to kick [themselves] at the end—rather than the author'. He also suggests that detachment was key to her achievement, as was her capacity to generate an atmosphere of 'trustful mistrust'. For Barnard, the reader approaches Christie with suspicion, while simultaneously feeling secure in the knowledge that they will not be cheated by her plotting. He also proposes answers to the question of why Christie has such international appeal. Her lack of specificity in character and setting, he argues, enables readers across the globe to populate the imaginative space with their own versions of what a religious hypocrite, a pompous businessman, a hyper-respectable matron, or a dangerous adventurer might look like. 'Christie', he continues, 'only seems to create a vision of England and English society; in fact she creates a broad, rather anonymous society on to which the reader can superimpose [their] own community'. To this we might add consideration of Christie's style: the economy of her prose matters, especially in the first decades of her career. Here, her dialogue-driven work avoids pinning down characters with descriptions or explanations, leaving them fresh for appropriation and interpretation by new readers. In telling us so little, she enables so much.

This conceptual translatability is important. As an explanation of Christie's success, it stands the test of time, and indeed seems endorsed by the continued growth of her global brand. But there are other factors at play in understanding the writing's ongoing appeal. Critics have long stressed the attraction of Christie's puzzle-focused storytelling: she is, Knight and Barnard argue, the logical successor to Conan Doyle. Yet, in terms of influence, she is equally the logical inheritor of Robert Louis Stevenson, and this literary lineage puts a rather different perspective on her success. Christie was undoubtedly familiar with Stevenson's *Strange Case of Dr Jekyll and Mr Hyde* (1886), and its symbolic attractions are made explicit in *Nemesis*: 'Jekyll and Hyde are real, you know', says a character attempting to explain an otherwise inexplicable act of violence (chapter 18). But the influence of Jekyll and Hyde goes further than such direct allusions. As a writer Christie is fascinated by duality, and by the social and psychic forces that necessitate the repression of desire. In Stevenson's novella, Dr Jekyll's downfall comes not from his 'certain gaiety of disposition' but from his 'imperious desire…to wear a more than commonly grave countenance before the public'. Christie's novels, from *Ackroyd* to *Endless Night*, reflect upon this performative self, and on the corrosive constraints of respectability. As Poirot puts it in *Mrs McGinty's Dead*: 'More murders have been committed for respectability than one would believe possible!' (chapter 11). A different appropriation of Stevenson is evident in the 'manuscript document' that ends *And Then There Were None*. 'I have a definite sadistic delight in seeing or causing death', writes Judge Wargrave, but 'side by side with this went a contradictory trait—a strong sense of justice'. He has been infinitely more successful than Henry Jekyll at balancing the needs of his divided self and, were it not for his desire to reveal his own cleverness, would have gone to his grave with his 'more than commonly grave countenance' intact.

That the influence of Stevenson is not so readily recognized as that of Doyle is perhaps down to structure. Stevenson encapsulated the radical duality of human nature, and the terror of losing control, into one short, vivid, and highly influential book; Christie spread it across a life's work. But their shared sensibility can be traced in a terror of what lies within, the perception that not just the other but the self is ultimately unknowable. This appeal—closer, as I suggested earlier, to domestic noir than to clue-puzzle detection—is at the heart of novels where characters lie because they cannot be sure that a loved one did not, in fact, commit the murder. It also, of course, structures those many novels where charming and attractive, or modest and unassuming, characters turn into Mr Hyde: *Peril at End House*, *Towards Zero*, *A Caribbean Mystery*, *Evil Under the Sun*, to name just a few. A 19th-century gothic sensibility also shapes Christie's actual monsters—domestic tyrants, manipulative lovers, and egotistical invalids—who vampirically drain the life and energy from those around them. The malignant Mrs Boynton in *Appointment with Death* (1938) is perhaps the most extreme example of updated gothic villainy. Mrs Boynton does not need to lock up her children, she mesmerizes them by willpower alone, taking sadistic pleasure in asserting not so much what she wants, as the opposite of whatever they want. The sense of menace she generates is immense, and the first part of the novel becomes a reflection on evil, a suspense-driven example of domestic noir; the second, after her murder, is a conventional dialogue-driven puzzle.

Appointment with Death provides two different Christies in one volume and gestures towards the need for multiple answers to the question of her ongoing popularity. 'Christie' as crime writer, novelist, and playwright is far from a unified phenomenon, and readers agreeing that they 'like' Agatha Christie might not be liking quite the same thing. Setting aside the different preoccupations of Mary Westmacott and the different discipline that shaped Christie on stage, comparing her most famous detectives hints towards the diversity of her output. Poirot is a cosmopolitan figure, uprooted from the outset, he is mobile, transient, and, for much of this career, distinctively modern. 'I belong to the world', he announces, grandly, in *Murder on the Orient Express* (part II, chapter 7). Belonging nowhere, he makes himself at home everywhere, bringing an outsider's eye to bear on the pathologies of the British at home and abroad. Miss Marple, by contrast, does belong somewhere—she is rooted in St Mary Mead and all that it might be expected to symbolize—but, equally, she is the antithesis of conventional structures of authority, the fantasy figure of the underestimated hero. She is also someone who tells us that the strange, the different, and the 'foreign' can all be assimilated within the parameters of village life. She is at pains to stress that this life is far from cosy—indeed, by her account it is replete with 'perversion of all kinds' (*A Caribbean Mystery*, chapter 1)—but it is not beyond our comprehension.

There are, then, distinctively different flavours to Marple and Poirot, and to the adventure stories and psychological thrillers. But what other attractions might Christie's writing offer to readers old and new? One answer lies in the ongoing appeal of her thematic preoccupations. Christie's fiction negotiates a series of surprisingly modern anxieties around truth, lies, and privacy, and her handling of these concerns can be read as refreshingly non-judgemental. The assumption that 'everyone lies' is integral to clue-puzzle structure, and an observation made regularly by Poirot; but in Christie's world some lies are more important than others, and people have a right to secrets. There are two modes of reassurance here. Poirot and Marple's uncanny discernment, their exceptional ability to tell truth from fiction, is a superpower appropriate to a post-truth age. Yet, they also recognize that truth is complicated, and its revelation will cause pain; as a result, lesser crimes and past misdeeds seldom go beyond the confessional space offered by the detective. As with truth, so with anonymity, and here by contrast Christie's fictions have a nostalgic appeal that might be connected to the exponential growth of historical detective fiction. The 20th century offered a freedom of movement and self-invention no longer available in a world of surveillance, DNA testing, mobile phones, and digital footprints; people could both disappear and reinvent themselves. Christie's fiction reactivates this fantasy. Beneath the fixity of social convention lies a remarkable fluidity: men and women can perform roles, erase their pasts, change their scripts. This is simultaneously a disorientating threat and a delicious fantasy of psycho-social mobility.

Another answer lies in the pleasure provided by Christie's women characters. Miss Marple is widely recognized as a radical empowerment of the despised spinster, and alongside her the books present women in a refreshing diversity of roles. Christie creates women who are clever, foolish, plucky, resourceful, timid, subservient, cantankerous, kind, vicious, and ironic, and when it comes to the business of murder, they all enjoy equal opportunity. Some of her types may now seem dated, but the active, insubordinate presence of her best women characters cuts across stereotypes and admits, however marginally, a frustration at the limitations placed upon women's lives. Christie was not what we might recognize as a feminist, but there is across her work a distinctive questioning of norms, and a characteristic non-alignment that keeps her writing fresh. This refusal to commit—a sort of ideological contrariness—is also evident in her ethical evasiveness. Evil is much talked about, especially in the later books, and the evidence suggests that Christie believed in such a concept, but she seldom deals in bogeymen and does not imagine that evil adheres to types or backgrounds. Rather, she sees evil acts—crimes committed through possessiveness, egotism, and pride—and the corrosive legacy they leave behind. She is quite capable of sympathizing with perpetrators as well as victims, even if she has no qualms about executing the guilty.

Christie's ethical capaciousness is shared by Hercule Poirot. He 'does not approve of murder', but he is willing to overlook pretty much everything else. As a result, Christie's novels are full of characters who make mistakes and get away with it, or are forgiven or redeemed. It is a comfortable dimension to her otherwise disturbing fictions, but that it seldom becomes sentimental can be attributed to Christie's distanced tone and sense of humour—a feature of her writing that deserves more attention. Humour takes multiple forms across the work. Miss Marple's wry pessimism about the human condition is situationally funny, as are her encounters with her highbrow nephew Raymond. Modernist prose is parodied, as—through the travails of Mrs Oliver—is Christie's own crime writing. Poirot is an object of humour, ridiculed by his creator, but he also enjoys the pleasure of making jokes, usually at Hastings' expense. Pastiche plays a role—in the *Partners in Crime* short stories—and Christie enjoyed playing with genre form, turning the seriousness of the male thriller into a showcase for clever young women who get the better of pompous, opinionated men. Above all, though, she excelled at social satire. Christie's observational humour—applied across the social spectrum—brings light relief to her more serious fictions and generates witty sketches which illustrate that effective characterization does not necessarily have to be 'deep'.

Agatha Christie's writing is, thus, more diverse, more complex, and more attractive than her long-standing reputation as a constructor of puzzles suggests. Alison Light made this clear in her argument that Christie's interwar fiction provided 'a modern sense of the unstable limits of respectability', and later critics have endorsed and developed this insight. J. C. Bernthal recognizes a queer embrace of ambivalence, a 'critical edge' that enables both a playful refusal of absolutes and a relentless questioning of normative structures; Alistair Rolls and Jesper Gulddal describe her as a writer 'given to textual perversity, flaunting conventions as often as respecting them and tirelessly reworking detective fiction'. Christie is also important as a chronicler of the 20th century, a figure whose most successful work marries modernist and middlebrow influences to create a distinctive middle-class English prose style. I have argued, along with Light and Bernthal, that her work is acutely attuned to the tenor of the times, something that emerges in her adaption of genre forms rather than a direct engagement with contemporary politics. Christie responds to social change through allusion and gesture; she gives us unparalleled insight into the structures of feeling shaping the vast expanse of the mid-century middle classes.

Yet, for all that her work is rooted in 20th-century preoccupations, the anxieties that Christie mobilizes are not purely historical. Her fiction translates across age and generation, across temporal as well as spatial boundaries. We recognize each novel as of its time, but the emotional force—the pressures and pleasures that drive plot and character—still resonates. People still commit murder for money; they still suffer the pain of jealousy; they still wish to hide socially unacceptable or criminal desires behind a façade of respectability. Forget serial killers: it is still the case that you are most likely to be murdered by someone close to you.

The ultimate inscrutability of self and other is at best a partial answer to the question of why Christie's writing appeals, but it does gesture towards a critical duality. Suspect everyone, question everything, doubt yourself. To 'get' Christie we need to supplement Barnard's eloquent reading of 'trustful mistrust' with a recognition of her emotional intelligence. Alongside her capacity to puzzle, Christie's fiction creates a disorientating state of psycho-social unease. Her belief, reiterated across her entire career, that people are 'not quite bad or quite good' (*Taken at the Flood*, chapter 2) asks readers to accept ambivalence and to live with the knowledge that who *actually* committed murder matters less than the recognition that anyone *could* have. 'Nothing's safe' says the dangerously attractive, risk-taking ex-soldier David Hunter in *Taken at the Flood* (chapter 4), and there may be no better way of encapsulating the threat—and the pleasure—of Christie's fictional world.

References

A full list of Christie's novels can be found in any current or recent HarperCollins edition. Details of all her writing, including the plays and more recent continuation fiction, can be found online at: https://www.agathachristie.com/

Chapter 1: Agatha Christie and the 'Golden Age' of crime

Agatha Christie, *An Autobiography* (HarperCollins, 1993 [1977]).

Janet Morgan, *Agatha Christie: A Biography* (HarperCollins, 1997 [1984]).

Laura Thompson, *Agatha Christie: An English Mystery* (Headline Review, 2007).

Lucy Worsley, *Agatha Christie: A Very Elusive Woman* (Hodder & Stoughton, 2022).

Jared Cade, *Agatha Christie and the Eleven Missing Days* (Peter Owen, 1998).

Julius Green, *Agatha Christie—A Life in Theatre* (HarperCollins, 2015).

Alison Light, *Forever England: Femininity, Literature and Conservatism Between the Wars* (Routledge, 1991).

Raymond Chandler, 'The Simple Art of Murder', *Pearls are a Nuisance* (Penguin, 1964 [1950]).

Ronald A. Knox, 'A Detective Story Decalogue', in Howard Haycraft (ed.), *The Art of the Mystery Story* (Carroll and Graf, 1992 [1946]).

S. S. Van Dine, 'Twenty Rules for Writing Detective Stories', in Howard Haycraft (ed.), *The Art of the Mystery Story* (Carroll and Graf, 1992 [1946]).

W. H. Auden, 'The Guilty Vicarage', *The Dyer's Hand and Other Essays* (Faber, 1975 [1963]).

Sigmund Freud, 'Thoughts for the Times on War and Death', in James Strachey (ed.), *The Standard Edition of the Complete Psychological Works of Sigmund Freud*, Vol. XIV, 1915 (Hogarth, 1957).

'enigmatic and arresting personality' (Christie 1993: 14)

'in love with her own childhood' (Thompson 2007: 1)

'her voice defeated her' (Morgan 1997: 47)

'a stranger' (Christie 1993: 223)

'had the happy attitude…' (Christie 1993: 227)

'an easy touch when he saw one' (Thompson 2007: 119)

'the complete amateur…' (Christie 1993: 227)

'for the middle classes' (Morgan 1997: 81)

'I ought to have felt misgiving' (Christie 1993: 346)

'configures the breakdown of her marriage' (Christie 1993: 346)

'I can't stand not having what I want' (Christie 1993: 363)

'wishful thinking, zealous speculation' (Morgan 1997: 156–7)

'She draws heavily on Christie's fictions' (Morgan 1997: 218)

'dissociative fugue' (Worsley 2022: 129)

'Jared Cade describes a revenge plot' (Cade 1998: 120–4)

'great rupture of 1926' (Thompson 2007: 260)

'Archie's deals in the City' (Christie 1993: 430)

'free of outside shadows' (Christie 1993: 483)

'So time went on' (Christie 1993: 506)

'intellectually demanding but safe' (Morgan 1997: 294)

'the most successful female playwright of all time' (Green 2015: 1)

'With glowing reviews' (Green 2015: 384–90)

'tentacle of British soft power in the region' (Worsley 2022: 272)

'married woman' (Christie 1993: 445)

'at Nineveh, where she overcame' (Christie 1993: 470)

'A deal with MGM' (Morgan 1997: 337)

'I often feel that it might be as well' (Christie 1993: 427)

'Morgan suggests she retained' (Morgan 1997: 363)

'written in three intensive days' (Christie 1993: 517)

'the one book that has satisfied me completely' (Christie 1993: 516)

'The English may not always' (Chandler 1964: 191)

'revolutionary debunking' (Chandler 1964: 194)

'Hammett gave murder back' (Chandler 1964: 195)

'nothing is sacred' (Light 1991: 67)

'a literature of convalescence' (Light 1991: 69)

'no lesser crime than murder will suffice' (Van Dine 1992: 190)

'a murder occurs' (Auden 1975: 147)
'a genius from outside' (Auden 1975: 158)
'What no human soul desires' (Freud 1957: 296)
'if we are to be judged' (Freud 1957: 297)
'Thriller plays are usually much alike' (Christie 1993: 448–9)
'tradesman in a good honest trade' (Christie 1993: 345)

Chapter 2: Means, motive, and opportunity: Christie's techniques

Stephen Knight, *Form and Ideology in Crime Fiction* (Macmillan, 1980).
Ronald A. Knox, 'A Detective Story Decalogue', in Howard Haycraft
(ed.), *The Art of the Mystery Story* (Carroll and Graf, 1992 [1946]).
Pierre Bayard, *Who Killed Roger Ackroyd? The Mystery Behind the
Agatha Christie Mystery* (The New Press, 2000 [1998]).
John Curran, *Agatha Christie's Secret Notebooks* (Harper, 2010
[2009]).
J. C. Bernthal, *Queering Agatha Christie: Revisiting the Golden Age
of Detective Fiction* (Palgrave, 2016).
Alison Light, *Forever England, Femininity, Literature and
Conservatism Between the Wars* (Routledge, 1991).
'an imitatable method' (Knight 1980: 109)
'must not conceal any thoughts' (Knox 1992: 196)
'[W]ith each reader mapping' (Bayard 2000: 69)
'most effective ploys' (Curran 2010: 39)
'a self-conscious frailty in all' (Bernthal 2016: 8, 14)
'refusal of seriousness' (Light 1991: 68)
'Yet she was also an evasive writer' (Curran 2010: 427–30)

Chapter 3: Not just escapism? Christie in context

Alison Light, *Forever England, Femininity, Literature and
Conservatism Between the Wars* (Routledge, 1991).
Merja Makinen, *Agatha Christie: Investigating Femininity*
(Palgrave, 2006).
Jane Waller and Michael Vaughan-Rees, *Women in Wartime: The Role
of Women's Magazines 1939–1945* (MacDonald Optima, 1987).
Sonya O. Rose, *Which People's War? National Identity and Citizenship
in Wartime Britain 1939–1945* (Oxford University Press, 2003).
Michal Shapira, *The War Inside: Psychoanalysis, Total War, and the
Making of the Democratic Self in Postwar Britain* (Cambridge
University Press, 2013).

Stephen Knight, 'Murder in Wartime', in Pat Kirkham and David Thoms (eds), *War Culture: Social Change and Changing Experience in World War Two* (Lawrence & Wishart, 1995).

Christie business papers, Exeter University Library (Denver Lindley at Colliers, letter to Harold Ober, 28 December 1942).

'critics suggest that her writing reveals' (Light 1991: 64; Makinen 2006: 1)

'Beauty is your Duty!' (Waller and Vaughan-Rees 1987: 80)

'temperate masculinity' (Rose 2003: 195)

'domestic citizens' (Shapira 2013: 113)

'disruptions to the normal balance' (Knight 1995: 163)

'that love and marriage would follow' (Rose 2003: 128)

'a significant public apprehension' (Rose 2003: 124)

Chapter 4: Criminal opinions? Christie's politics

Edmund Wilson, 'Who Cares Who Killed Roger Ackroyd?', in Howard Haycraft (ed.), *The Art of the Mystery Story* (Carroll & Graf, 1992 [1946]).

Gillian Gill, *Agatha Christie: The Woman and Her Mysteries* (Robson Books, 1991).

Agatha Christie, *An Autobiography* (HarperCollins, 1993 [1977]).

George Orwell, 'Antisemitism in Britain', in Sonia Orwell and Ian Angus (eds), *The Collected Essays, Journalism and Letters of George Orwell, Vol III, As I Please, 1943–1945* (Penguin, 1970 [1968]).

Nadia Atia, 'Christie's Contemporary Middle East', in Mary Anna Evans and J. C. Bernthal (eds), *The Bloomsbury Handbook to Agatha Christie* (Bloomsbury, 2023).

Judy Suh, 'Agatha Christie in the American Century', in *Studies in Popular Culture*, 39:1, fall 2016.

Christopher Prior, 'An Empire Gone Bad: Agatha Christie, Anglocentrism and Decolonization', in *Cultural and Social History*, 15:2, 2018.

Meta G. Carstarphen, 'Of Race, Law, and Order: Colonial Ghosts', in Evans and Bernthal (eds), *The Bloomsbury Handbook to Agatha Christie* (Bloomsbury, 2023).

Clare Hanson, *Eugenics, Literature and Culture in Post-war Britain* (Routledge, 2013).

J. C. Bernthal, *Queering Agatha Christie: Revisiting the Golden Age of Detective Fiction* (Palgrave, 2016).

'who cares who killed Roger Ackroyd?' (Wilson 1992: 395)

'stupidly unthinking' (Gill 1991: 91)

'himself wholly supportive of the Nazi agenda' (Christie 1993: 482)

'observes that antisemitism, while widespread' (Orwell 1970: 382)

'conform closely to the expectations of her readership (Atia 2023: 166)

'celebration of ordinary, workaday domestic life' (Suh 2016: 72)

'people are the same whatever century' (Christie 1993: 513)

'trenchant support for executing those who kill' (Christie 1993: 453–4)

'tainted with the germs of ruthlessness and hatred' (Christie 1993: 454)

'racist imaginary' (Carstarphen 2023: 199)

'still possible to argue that the poor' (Hanson 2013: 67)

'frailty of contemporary normality' (Bernthal 2016: 201–2)

Chapter 5: Adaptation and afterlives

Janet Morgan, *Agatha Christie: A Biography* (HarperCollins, 1997 [1984]).

Kathleen Glasgow and Liz Lawson, *The Agathas* (Rock the Boat, 2022).

Mark Aldridge, *Agatha Christie on Screen* (Palgrave Macmillan, 2016).

Julius Green, *Agatha Christie—A Life in Theatre* (HarperCollins, 2015).

Agatha Christie, *The Mousetrap and Other Plays* (HarperCollins, 2011).

Linda Hutcheon with Siobhan O'Flynn, *A Theory of Adaptation*, 2nd edition (Routledge, 2012).

Sarah Phelps, interviewed for the BBC podcast series *Inside the Writers Room*, 3 August 2017.

Robert Barnard, *A Talent to Deceive: An Appreciation of Agatha Christie* (Fontana, 1990 [1980]).

Robert Louis Stevenson, *The Strange Case of Dr Jekyll and Mr Hyde* (Penguin, 1979 [1886]).

Alison Light, *Forever England, Femininity, Literature and Conservatism Between the Wars* (Routledge, 1991).

J. C. Bernthal, *Queering Agatha Christie: Revisiting the Golden Age of Detective Fiction* (Palgrave, 2016).

Alistair Rolls and Jesper Gulddal, 'Introduction', *Clues*, 34:1, spring 2016.

Gill Plain '"Tale Engineering": Agatha Christie and the Aftermath of the Second World War', in *Literature and History*, 29:2, 2020.

'[T]o Rosalind now fell the task' (Morgan 1997: 376–7)
'greatly distressed' (Aldridge 2016: 104)
'the success of Rutherford in the role' (Aldridge 2016: 95)
'This film saw the transition of Christie' (Aldridge 2016: 122)
'end up observing the detective' (Green 2015: 79)
'Christie's theatrical peak was reached' (Green 2015: 414)
He is an attractive, lean man of thirty-four (Christie 2011: 5)
'hilarious chiller thriller' (Green 2015: 189)
'repetition with variation' (Hutcheon 2012: 4, 8)
'wonderful simplicity' (Barnard 1990: 38)
'trustful mistrust' (Barnard 1990: 67)
'only seems to create a vision' (Barnard 1990: 112)
'certain gaiety of disposition' (Stevenson: 81)
'a modern sense of the unstable limits of respectability' (Light
    1991: 61)
'critical edge' (Bernthal 2016: 201)
'given to textual perversity' (Rolls and Gulddal 2016: 9)

Further reading

The most comprehensive biographical accounts of Christie's life and times are those of Janet Morgan and Laura Thompson. Lucy Worsley's more recent book is less detailed overall, but a lively read with an excellent collection of photographs. Another useful account is provided by Gillian Gill's literary biography, *Agatha Christie: The Woman and Her Mysteries* (Portico, 1999). Jared Cade's *Agatha Christie and the Eleven Missing Days* (Peter Owen, 1998) reads Christie's life through the prism of 1926. Christie's other life as a playwright is the subject of Julius Green's substantial and informative *Agatha Christie: A Life in Theatre* (HarperCollins, 2015); the book also provides a counterhistory of British theatre, chronicling the story of populist drama and those who produced, directed, and financed it. A parallel history of adaptations is provided by Mark Aldridge's compendious *Agatha Christie on Screen* (Palgrave, 2016). More recently, Aldridge has produced richly detailed cultural histories of Poirot (2020) and Marple (2024). The characters of Poirot and Marple are now so successful that they have biographies of their own, both by Anne Hart. There are in addition five Poirot continuation novels by Sophie Hannah, and a new book of short stories featuring Miss Marple (HarperCollins, 2022).

Critical accounts combining life and work include Robert Barnard's *A Talent to Deceive*, which rather undersells itself as 'an appreciation'. It offers a perceptive introduction to Christie and an acute analysis of her techniques. A snapshot of Christie's status in the 1970s is provided by the impressive array of crime writers who contributed to H. R. F. Keating's *Agatha Christie: First Lady of Crime* (1977).

The book has been reissued with a new introduction by Sophie Hannah (Weidenfeld & Nicolson, 2020). An intimate sense of Christie's writing process can be gleaned from her notebooks, two volumes of which have been edited by John Curran (*Agatha Christie's Secret Notebooks*, HarperCollins, 2009; and *Agatha Christie's Murder in the Making*, HarperCollins, 2012). Curran has also produced *Tom Adams Uncovered: The Art of Agatha Christie and Beyond* (HarperCollins, 2015), an account of the remarkable cover art that made the design of the Fontana paperbacks in the 1960s and 1970s so distinctive. A fascinating alternative approach to Christie history is provided by Kathryn Harkup, *A Is for Arsenic: The Poisons of Agatha Christie* (Bloomsbury Sigma, 2015).

Christie is also integral to studies of 20th-century crime fiction. Key interventions that demanded she be taken seriously include Stephen Knight's *Form and Ideology in Crime Fiction* (Macmillan, 1980); Alison Light's *Forever England: Femininity, Literature and Conservatism Between the Wars* (Routledge, 1991); Marion Shaw and Sabine Vanacker's *Reflecting on Miss Marple* (Routledge, 1991). In the 21st century, academic interest in Christie's work has increased dramatically. For her engagement with gender and women's lives, see Susan Rowland, *From Agatha Christie to Ruth Rendell* (Palgrave, 2001); Merja Makinen, *Agatha Christie: Investigating Femininity* (Palgrave, 2006); Megan Hoffman, *Gender and Representation in British 'Golden Age' Crime Fiction* (Palgrave, 2016); and Gill Plain, 'Death on the Roads: Motoring with Agatha Christie', *Crime Fiction Studies*, 5:1, 2024; for her approach to ethics and evil, see R. A. York, *Agatha Christie: Power and Illusion* (Palgrave, 2007), Heta Pyrhönen, *Mayhem and Murder: Narrative and Moral Issues in the Detective Story* (University of Toronto Press, 2016), and Fiona Peters, 'Agatha Christie: Evil, Love and Desire', *Crime Fiction Studies*, 3:2, 2022.

J. C. Bernthal, in *Queering Agatha Christie: Revisiting the Golden Age of Detective Fiction* (Palgrave, 2016), examines the challenge her work presents to conventional family and relationship structures. Her responses to war are discussed in Gill Plain, *Twentieth Century Crime Fiction* (Edinburgh University Press, 2001) and J. C. Bernthal and Rebecca Mills (eds), *Agatha Christie Goes to War* (Routledge, 2020). Bernthal has also edited *The Ageless Agatha Christie* (McFarland, 2016) and, with Mary Anna Evans, *The Bloomsbury Handbook to*

Agatha Christie (Bloomsbury, 2022). This collection includes essays on religion, the state, justice, feminism, the Middle East, Christie's radio broadcasts, and her Westmacott novels. For archaeology, empire, and the Middle East, see Max Mallowan, *Mallowan's Memoirs: Agatha and the Archaeologist* (HarperCollins, 2010 [1977]); Billie Melman, *Empires of Antiquities: Modernity and the Rediscovery of the Ancient Near East* (Oxford University Press, 2020); Phyllis Lassner, in Robin Hackett et al. (eds), *At Home and Abroad: British Women Write the 1930s* (University of Delaware Press, 2009); Christopher Prior, 'An Empire Gone Bad: Agatha Christie, Anglocentrism and Decolonization', in *Cultural and Social History*, 15:2, 2018; and Judy Suh, 'Agatha Christie in the American Century', *Studies in Popular Culture*, 39:1, fall 2016.

Starting with Pierre Bayard's *Who Killed Roger Ackroyd?* (The New Press, 2000 [1998]), there has been a growing critical literature exploring the instability of the supposedly 'closed' detective novel. See Jesper Gulddal, '"Beautiful Shining Order": Detective Authority in Agatha Christie's *Murder on the Orient Express*', in *Clues*, 34:1, 2016; and '"That Deep Underground Savage Instinct": Narratives of Sacrifice and Retribution in Agatha Christie's *Appointment with Death*', in *Textual Practice*, 34:11, 2020; Chris Ewers, 'Genre in Transit: Agatha Christie, Trains, and the Whodunit', in *Journal of Narrative Theory*, 46:1, 2016; and Alastair Rolls, *Agatha Christie and New Directions in Reading Detective Fiction: Narratology and Detective Criticism* (Routledge, 2022). The special issue of *Clues*, 'Reappropriating Agatha Christie', cited above, also includes essays on the role of playfulness, self-referentiality, and parody in her fiction.

Dorothy L. Sayers' thoughts on the 'love interest' in crime fiction can be found in her introduction to the *Omnibus of Crime* (1928), reprinted in Howard Haycraft (ed.), *The Art of the Mystery Story* (Simon and Schuster, 1946). This compendium of early critical essays on the form also contains Raymond Chandler's 'The Simple Art of Murder', first published in the *Atlantic Monthly* (1944); and Edmund Wilson's 'Who Cares Who Killed Roger Ackroyd?', reprinted from the *New Yorker* (1945). More recent accounts of the Golden Age formula, its contexts, and history are provided by: John G. Cawelti, *Adventure, Mystery and Romance: Formula Stories as Art and Popular Culture* (University of Chicago Press, 1977); Martin Priestman, *The Cambridge*

Companion to Crime Fiction (Cambridge University Press, 2003); Lee Horsley, *Twentieth-Century Crime Fiction* (Oxford University Press, 2005); Stephen Knight, *Crime Fiction since 1800: Detection, Death, Diversity*, 2nd edition (Palgrave, 2010); John Scaggs, *Crime Fiction* (Routledge, 2005); and Victoria Stewart, *Crime Writing in Interwar Britain: Fact and Fiction in the Golden Age* (Cambridge University Press, 2017).

Index

C

D

E

Agatha Christie

BESTSELLERS
A Very Short Introduction
John Sutherland

'I rejoice', said Doctor Johnson, 'to concur with the Common Reader.' For the last century, the tastes and preferences of the common reader have been reflected in the American and British bestseller lists, and this *Very Short Introduction* takes an engaging look through the lists to reveal what we have been reading - and why. John Sutherland shows that bestseller lists monitor one of the strongest pulses in modern literature and are therefore worthy of serious study. Along the way, he lifts the lid on the bestseller industry, examines what makes a book into a bestseller, and asks what separates bestsellers from canonical fiction.

'His amiable trawl through the history of popular books is frequently entertaining'

Scott Pack, The Times

www.oup.com/vsi

ENGLISH LITERATURE

A Very Short Introduction

Jonathan Bate

Sweeping across two millennia and every literary genre, acclaimed scholar and biographer Jonathan Bate provides a dazzling introduction to English Literature. The focus is wide, shifting from the birth of the novel and the brilliance of English comedy to the deep Englishness of landscape poetry and the ethnic diversity of Britain's Nobel literature laureates. It goes on to provide a more in-depth analysis, with close readings from an extraordinary scene in King Lear to a war poem by Carol Ann Duffy, and a series of striking examples of how literary texts change as they are transmitted from writer to reader.

{No reviews}

www.oup.com/vsi

ENGLISH LANGUAGE
A Very Short Introduction
Simon Horobin

The English language is spoken by more than a billion people throughout the world. But where did English come from? And how has it evolved into the language used today?

In this *Very Short Introduction* Simon Horobin investigates how we have arrived at the English we know today, and celebrates the way new speakers and new uses mean that it continues to adapt. Engaging with contemporary concerns about correctness, Horobin considers whether such changes are improvements, or evidence of slipping standards. What is the future for the English language? Will Standard English continue to hold sway, or we are witnessing its replacement by newly emerging Englishes?

www.oup.com/vsi

Modernism
A Very Short Introduction
Christopher Butler

Whether we recognise it or not, virtually every aspect of our life today has been influenced in part by the aesthetic legacy of Modernism. In this *Very Short Introduction* Christopher Butler examines how and why Modernism began, explaining what it is and showing how it has gradually informed all aspects of 20th and 21st century life. Butler considers several aspects of modernism including some modernist works; movements and notions of the avant garde; and the idea of 'progress' in art. Butler looks at modernist ideas of the self, subjectivity, irrationalism, people and machines, and political definitions of modernism as a whole.

www.oup.com/vsi

WRITING AND SCRIPT
A Very Short Introduction
Andrew Robinson

Without writing, there would be no records, no history, no
books, and no emails. Writing is an integral and essential part
of our lives; but when did it start? Why do we all write differently
and how did writing develop into what we use today? All of
these questions are answered in this *Very Short Introduction*.
Starting with the origins of writing five thousand years ago,
with cuneiform and Egyptian hieroglyphs, Andrew Robinson
explains how these early forms of writing developed into
hundreds of scripts including the Roman alphabet and the
Chinese characters.

'User-friendly survey.'

Steven Poole, The Guardian

www.oup.com/vsi

Logic
A Very Short Introduction
Graham Priest

Logic is often perceived as an esoteric subject, having little
to do with the rest of philosophy, and even less to do with real life.
In this lively and accessible introduction, Graham Priest shows
how wrong this conception is. He explores the philosophical
roots of the subject, explaining how modern formal logic deals
with issues ranging from the existence of God and the reality
of time to paradoxes of self-reference, change, and probability.
Along the way, the book explains the basic ideas of formal
logic in simple, non-technical terms, as well as the philosophical
pressures to which these have responded. This is a book for
anyone who has ever been puzzled by a piece of reasoning.

'a delightful and engaging introduction to the basic concepts of
logic. Whilst not shirking the problems, Priest always manages to
keep his discussion accessible and instructive.'

Adrian Moore, St Hugh's College, Oxford

'an excellent way to whet the appetite for logic. . . . Even if you read
no other book on modern logic but this one, you will come away
with a deeper and broader grasp of the *raison d'être* for logic.'

Chris Mortensen, University of Adelaide